D1450524

Sebastian & Me,

A Rite of Passage and Spiritual Journey

Storm:

Believe in the Power of
your Dreams!

Kay A. Clark

By Kay A. Clark

Preface

If you love animals and especially if you are a cat owner, I believe you will enjoy this book of short stories on the delightful adventures and antics of two of God's endearing and furry creatures. What started out as a journal on how I coped with the absence of Sebastian, my beloved orange cat, developed into much more. Being a feral cat at birth, he had a lot of pent up energy and curiosity that couldn't be contained. When he came up missing for several days, I began recording my search along with all of the questions we all ask ourselves when left alone with our own thoughts. My discoveries turned out to be a spiritual journey of faith for me and a rite of passage for him. And then we both opened our hearts and home to another beautiful feline, Sidney.

I hope you enjoy reading about their escapades and how they came to be 'best buds' and the loves of my life.

Acknowledgements

*I would like to thank Mrs. Barbara McKenzie, my junior
high school English teacher; Bea Goke, a good friend who
encouraged my writing skill; Sandy Gentile, Barbara Rayford
Sallee, Linda Wenzel and many other friends who thought I
had a way with words.*

*I am particularly grateful to the Algonquin Area Writers
Group for their organization and constructive critiques of
my work that helped affirm and gave me the confidence to do
something with my writing ability.*

*Chris and Erika La Pelusa—Chris is the owner and managing
editor along with his wife, Erika, of the Sun Day newspaper
printed and distributed throughout the Sun City community
of Huntley, Illinois. Chris invited me to be a reporter for
the paper as well as the occasional photographer of the
interviewees. Through the numerous assignments he has given
me in interviewing and writing articles for the bi-monthly
paper, I have grown my skills as a writer of material that
people look forward to and enjoy reading. I would be remiss
if I didn't acknowledge their thoughtful care and concern for
Sebastian. Thank you so much, you two.*

*I would also thank Carolyn Batzlaff, a fellow member of the
writing group, author, and good friend who encouraged me
to meet a November challenge. She continues to support
me in my writing endeavors and I sincerely appreciate her
enthusiasm. Thank you, Carol!*

*Jerry Simm, another member of the writers group, gave me
the best advice when he said, "write what you know." Thanks,
Jerry.*

*The greatness of a nation and
its moral progress can be judged by the way
its animals are treated.*

Mahatma Gandhi

(1869-1948)

*There are two means of refuge
from the miseries of life: music and cats.*

Albert Schweitzer

(1875-1965)

*Thousands of years ago,
cats were worshipped as gods.
Cats have never forgotten this.*

Anonymous

When they are among us, cats are angels.

George Sand

(1804-1876)

Contents

My New Love

Enter—Sebastian!

My new Roommate

What greater gift than the love of a cat?
Charles Dickens

It was the fall of 2008 and I was still unemployed. The local library was alive with patrons doing research or catching up on their reading while I was pouring over the want ads of the daily paper. As I skimmed the ads, three of them popped out at me—"FREE KIT-TENS," "FREE KITTENS," and "FREE KITTENS" each one read with phone numbers attached. I had never seen three of them one right after the other like that. Was this an omen?

Having lived alone in a small apartment for over a year, I thought I had grown comfortable in my skin but somehow felt the Universe pulling on my heart strings. Or were my angels helping me heal with an animate object of unconditional love? I made note of the numbers and headed home. Hmmm…that would mean cat hair, litter boxes. Oh, let's go for it, I thought as I would welcome a furry companion.

With apprehension I dialed the first number. No answer. I dialed the second number and a lady answered. Could I come see her kittens? She informed me there were five kittens; two mothers, and a grandmother. She went on to tell me how old they were and their colors. Remembering my allergies, I asked if I might come and spend some time with them to see if I had a reaction to any of them. I had learned that I didn't always have a reaction and the reaction actually came from their saliva.

"Sure! Come on out! I'll be home this afternoon." Kathy was quite cordial and enthusiastically looked forward to my visit.

I made note of her address and she gave me the directions to her farm outside of Woodstock. I didn't have a GPS at this time. As I approached her home, I recognized the Fire number and turned onto the dirt and gravel drive that brought me to the back of the house. I got out of the car and walked up to the back door, knocked and a short, middle-aged lady came out to greet me. I noticed a few older cats were frolicking near the house running around the bushes. This was a farm and they were free to roam. And they loved every minute of it.

"Hi! Let me show you the kittens," Kathy cheerfully greeted me.

She went to the side of the cement patio and flipped the blue, stiff tarp back from the large wooden box exposing five very lively, colorful kittens. They welcomed the fresh air and immediately scampered here and there chasing and tumbling over one another in their scurry to keep up with the others. "Mew, Mew, Mew," their chorus played. They were so full of life, and so adorable. My heart melted and my face lit up just watching these little fur balls dart here and there over the landscaped lawn and racing around and behind the bushes.

Several moments went by as we visited and observed the kittens at play. The skies were overcast and there was a cool breeze but the babes didn't seem to mind. Soon one scampered up a nearby apple tree with another younger one vigorously following close behind.

Carefully checking out this menagerie, I focused my sights on an orange tabby that seemed to be a little more mature and observant of the antics of the others. Kathy informed me this little guy's name was 'Taffy.' She favored 'Taffy' as he would follow her to the barn and all around the barnyard.

However, he would soon take up permanent residence in my heart…and my home.

She went on to explain that shortly after the other kittens had been born, one day when she flipped the tarp back she counted SIX kittens!

"Well, where did YOU come from?" Kathy went on with her story. Apparently 'Taffy' had been born behind another building on the property possibly in June or July and just decided to join the others one day. She figured that's why 'Taffy' seemed to be a little more mature.

I could see that he was an observer of sorts and since I'm an 'observer,' we had something in common right away. Kathy invited me inside and offered me some tea as we continued our visit. A couple of kittens followed us into the kitchen. 'Taffy' was one of them.

I learned Kathy was a retired school teacher and she and her husband, Roger, had retired from farming but still lived on the farm. Every spring she would have another fresh litter of kittens to wean and offer up to loving homes. I could see she enjoyed her position of temporary guardian of these colorful furry angels so full of life and love. They were so darned cute and tiny. You just wanted to hold them and nestle them against your cheek feeling their soft fur.

My allergies seemed to be in check; no reaction. I was good to 'go.'

After an hour or so, it was time to make my selection and get to know my new roommate on a more intimate level. Bidding farewell to Kathy, I placed 'Taffy' in a box. Once inside the car, this enclosure was no challenge for 'Taffy,' as she quickly escaped and began roaming the inside of the car before we were out of the driveway. By this time we had run out of daylight and as we made our way home we met several cars each with a pair of bright lights; something 'Taffy' wasn't used to seeing. I sensed her anxiety as she quickly climbed onto my left shoulder and nestled next to my neck. With my right hand on the steering wheel, I tried to comfort her with my left hand assuring her she was safe and would be home soon.

Now to pick a name for her.

I didn't particularly like 'Taffy' and the only name that came to mind was 'Precious.' She purred all the way home; sweet music to my ears. I soon found myself gushing warm words of endearment to this beautifully marked, affectionate feline.

Once 'home,' she wandered all over the condo getting her bearings and checking out her new surroundings. I didn't force my affections onto her and just let her settle in for the night. There were lots of surfaces for her to nestle on. There were the two couches, a bed, and, of course, the counter, a bar stool next to the bedroom window for perching on, a rocking chair and all kinds of room on the carpeted flooring. With a southern exposure and full sun during the day, she would soon discover another favorite spot to stretch out and languish on.

"Well, good morning, sweetheart." I greeted her the next morning as she had camped out at the foot of my bed. She began her purring again and I purred back at her.

One morning, as it was a little chilly in the bedroom, I had my head partially buried under the covers. I opened my sleepy eyes at the sound of her 'wake up' trill and saw this beautiful, friendly face with two large eyes drawing closer to me. Soon, a paw was outstretched and tapped my face. I guess she didn't want to greet the day alone. Not quite. Actually, she was just hungry and put me on alert.

After a few days, 'Precious' didn't seem to fit and then I learned this kitten was a male. In my excitement I forgot. I typed in "Orange Tabby Cat Names" on the Internet and sure enough out of some fifty names; I narrowed my selection down to 'Sebastian.' Not Butterscotch, not Garfield, but Sebastian. I thought he would 'wear' that name very well. It was distinctive. He could roam proudly; strut his stuff, as they say. He would command respect in all of kitten-dom. It sounded regal and of prominence.

'Sebastian' it was. Of the Top 20 Male Cat Names, Sebastian came in 19.

Being a feral cat, he was quite lively and very curious. Any surface that proved interesting, and out of reach, he would spring up to it and if something was in the way, oh well... The bookshelves, the top of the refrigerator, and then another leap and he was up on top of the cabinets looking down on his 'world' with the empowerment of a lion surveying his domain. I have a closet in both bedrooms and he took particular delight in scaling the dresser in one of them, then leaping up on the shelf and on top of a box where the fur on top of his head tickled the ceiling. Sometimes he would get down gracefully retracing his steps. At other times, he brought a box down with him. Sigh!

I would be at the bathroom sink and he would follow me in and jump up on the commode and then the vanity. Staring at the faucet and running water, he would creep down into the bowl and drink from the steady stream of water satisfying his thirst. When he was finished, I would carefully pick him up trying not to disturb his full belly and place him down on the floor again. He was such a little tyke.

In the kitchen when I would lean over to get something out of the lower cupboard, there he would be at my feet. And then there would be that infamous leap and he would be on my back. I guess I should have felt flattered that he felt that comfortable with me. He loved bounding onto higher places so he could get a better view.

The same thing would happen when I was doing laundry. He would jump up on my back and then get on the washer and walk around the open lid. He loved to leap into the dryer and roll around in the nice, fluffy, warm clothes and look up at me so contented as if to want to take up residence there. People would tell me to be careful and make sure he was out of the dryer when I closed the door but I really never had that problem. I mean, he was small, but he wouldn't burrow under the clothes. I would leave him alone and eventually he would get out. I'd just have to give the clean clothes an extra shake.

Bottle caps from water bottles left on the table or counter weren't there for long. For some reason, Sebastian was a bottle cap magnet and it was just moments before a paw would flick that bottle cap on the floor and then he'd jump down and play with it until it disappeared under the refrigerator or oven. Then I'd get out the ruler and do my best to retrieve it for him. When a cap would disappear under the oven drawer, I'd pull it open so he could get at it easier. This only served as an invitation for him to further explore the drawer. So he'd jump in and go way back beyond the drawer and find his prize. One time I left the drawer open because I knew he was back there underneath; after a time I figured he had gotten what he was after and began closing the drawer. All of a sudden there was an obstacle in the way that prevented me from closing it all the way—Sebastian was still back there exploring. With a little coaxing, he was soon out and about again. What a pill.

In the evening, when I was outstretched watching TV, Sebastian would walk up my arms and chest and settle on my shoulder. It wasn't long and I would bring him down into my arms so as to cradle him like a babe. He really enjoyed that. I think he might have missed his Mother and was very affectionate. He stole a little bit of my heart every day…and still does.

When I would be in the bathroom on the commode, he would get up on the rim of the tub between the shower curtain and liner. I could pretty well judge his position and would scratch the curtain with my finger which would excite him and he would try to bite me. He thought he was really doing something sneaky hiding behind the curtains, but I knew where he was. I read where you should try to play with your pet at least ten minutes a day, because as a young kitten in this case, he needed playtime and it strengthened the bond between you and your cat. He had lots of energy and would sometimes have a wild spurt and race from one bedroom, through the living room to the other bedroom and back again. You'd almost swear something was chasing him or he was chasing something, but he had this adrenalin rush that needed to be released. It wouldn't be long and he would be down for a long cat nap. Silly kitty, but oh, so cute.

In time, Sebastian was curling up next to my face at bedtime resting his head on my outstretched arm and we would be looking into one another's eyes as we drifted off to slumber land. When I awoke I would discover him nestled on my back. I guess he not only wanted to be close but wanted to feel me breathing. Still a babe at heart.

Since he'd been a feral cat and was used to his freedom, I would put him in the car and we'd go to the park just north of the apartment. It was also a preserve so there were a lot of trees and brush and a few paths winding their way through the clearing and up and down the hills. I'd park the car and he was more than anxious to get out and explore or pretend he was on the hunt. Sometimes I would sit on the picnic benches with my notebook and pen in hand taking notes while

Here he is napping and covering up his nose. This is a favorite pose of his. Or did you do something wrong? ***Sebastian?***

he played in the grass and then lose him in the heavy weeds. Some days we would walk along the paths and he was very good about staying close to me. He would either follow me or scamper ahead and then turn around to make sure I was still following him. Then he'd take off again.

There was a pond and a little wooden bridge that we would walk over to continue around the pond and follow the wide grassy path to get back to the parking lot and the car. He would stop every few feet and sniff out the thick brush hoping to find something, I didn't know what. So I would, in turn, wait for him to finish his investigation before he'd join me again and we'd continue our hike.

Finally we would find the car and if Sebastian wasn't ready to surrender his freedom, he'd venture off into another area of trees, long grasses and other wild plants. They almost beckoned him to further explore and discover what could be hidden or lurking behind the mass of growth that would engulf him soon after he launched from the mown clearing.

By this time I figured he still had a little more energy to release and patiently waited until he had exhausted his curiosities. It had been some time since he had been out on the farm and I didn't know how long his memory was. Sometimes it turned out to be very good, much to my consternation. At long last, I would have to physically comb thru the edge of this wooded haven and cajole my little frisky friend back to reality.

Once back in the car I would forgive him and we would make a stop at the drive thru at McDonald's where we would share an ice cream cone. After he got in his licks, I would wipe his lickings away and finish it for him. What a Mom! I had hoped this little treat would give him incentive to return to the car after our little romp in the park but it didn't always work out that way. After all, he is a cat and cats are independent. He hadn't been fixed yet so he was still full of energy and was free to fully exercise his snooper's license.

And Up the Chimney He Rose
A Harrowing Adventure

One must love a cat on its own terms.
Paul Gray

It was early December and the day was cooler than normal leading into an even colder evening. It was time to decorate the fireplace for the holidays. Sebastian had taken up residence for a couple of months now and had checked out the fireplace screen before, but tonight his curiosity got the best of him.

He approached the cage protecting the logs and with his front claws firmly planted among the metal grid, he was able to advance up and over and into the opening of the base of the fireplace. Ah, the pile of split logs looked so inviting. I felt powerless to grab him. I did not want to upset the grid and unleash the fireplace utensils. That would frighten Sebastian to the point of making him escape up the chimney even faster. All I could do was anxiously watch his adventure unfold.

After a thorough investigation, it was time to gingerly maneuver his way over the dried chunks of wood. As his curiosity mounted, so did my anxiety. He gazed longingly up into the darkness of the chimney. Oh, please, no, I thought. He established his footing along the walls of the blackened abyss and began to climb up thru the flue and out of sight. There was the sound of the flue being dislodged and snapping shut!

Good Grief, now what do I do? Had Sebastian's fate been sealed? Was he gone forever? Had he used up all of his nine lives all in one fell swoop? Would I have to involve the neighbor across the hall? Or call the local fire department? Would he meet up with another frightened and imprisoned critter? A bird? A squirrel? Would I have to rename him 'Blackie?'

I found a flashlight, removed all barriers and opened the flue. Peering up into the foreboding chimney, I flashed the light up into the blackened dungeon where lo and behold, I saw two frightened eyes reflect back at me. Sebastian called for help: "Meeeooooww."

"Come on down from there, you silly kitty," I sternly beckoned. "I'm not going up after you. You're on your own on this one buddy!"

Sebastian hesitated.

"Come on down, Sebastian."

After a few moments of trepidation, Sebastian realized he had no choice and with one paw outstretched, he began to slide and descend the wooden planks breaking his fall from grace.

"You're a mess!"

I took one look at my soot-covered kitty and trying to be the good 'kitty-mother,' whisked him into the shower. I grabbed the faucet and waited for the water to become temperate. I did my best to hold him. Right? Wrong! Not the smartest thing to do as soot is extremely light and powdery and when it gets wet it becomes a thick and gooey paste. Somehow I think Sebastian knew this. He fought me with a vengeance. With his hind claws, he gouged my shirt and left a neat little hole. He did not like the spray of water that was pelting his fur.

While still wrestling with him, I tried to put a spot of shampoo on to help loosen the powder and make him all clean again. Well, that wasn't a smooth move. I barely got the soap out of his coat when I could see I was losing ground. I grabbed a towel so he could at least scamper out of my arms and not be all dripping wet.

The hair dryer certainly wasn't a welcome aid as the noise scared the livin' b'jeebers out of him. I resorted to towel drying as best I could manage him and then spent the next hour or so with him nestled on my chest as I stretched out on the couch with me blowing and fluffing his fur dry. He seemed to be content and cooperative. I think the whole ordeal put a fright into him and he was just happy to

Here's my little Sebastian in December, 2008. He's about six months old here and cute as all get out. He was my 'Christmas Wrapping Assistant' that first year...ok, more or less my...'Supervisor.' He couldn't figure out which end of the ribbon to start on!

be out in the open once again—and alive. He began to purr again and this was a good sign.

The fireplace grate had been replaced. A string of small, bright, white lights were draped and strung along the top lending the only light to the living room, while we listened to soft Christmas tunes on the stereo. We were both a little frazzled from the adventure and needed a serious time-out.

"He was dressed all in red" (well, orange), "from his head to his foot" (paw) "and his clothes" (fur) "were all covered in ashes and soot." (Well, not completely covered, but enough to need attention.) "Laying a finger aside of his nose, 'Up! the Chimney he rose.'" Well, ok, the paw did not get to the nose, but you get the idea.

All I could do was shake my head at my little adventurer and be thankful that he stopped short of going any further up the chimney. I would have thought this harrowing adventure would have satisfied his yen to check out the inner sanctum of the chimney but this was only the FIRST time. One more investigative trip up through the flue and a short time later, he returned only not as sooty as before.

Since then, his curiosity has been satisfied and there have been no...more...trips...up the chimney. His nine lives are still intact. Or is he down to eight?

Sebastian and Kay's Excellent Adventure?

A Bonding Experience

A meow massages the heart.

Stuart McMillan

Sebastian was about seven months old and it was time to schedule an appointment with the vet to have him 'taken care of.' While he was there I thought I would also have his front claws removed. My new love seat was beginning to show wear from being his scratching post besides the one I already had for him, and I had a few scratches of my own to show for his play-time activities. The vet's office in my hometown, about three-and-a-half hours northwest up in Wisconsin, charged a much lower fee and also gave me an opportunity to visit with Dad, family and friends.

The surgery was scheduled for early Wednesday afternoon of January 14th, and we arrived in Platteville late that morning. The weather was rather chilly with more snow on the ground than in Illinois. I dropped Sebastian off at the office and bid him a fond goodbye. Sebastian might have thought, "I wonder what I'm in for now." But I knew he was in good hands and went back to Dad's. I was pleased he was going to be kept for two days. This way I could get in some quality visits.

Friday morning came and I received the call from the Vet's office that he was ready to be picked up. At first sight he appeared well and ready to resume his life but only in a different gear until he fully healed. The vet advised I replace his regular kitty litter with either newspaper shreds or oatmeal for at least a week to avoid any infection. I made sure to pick up two containers of oatmeal in pampering my patient to assist in his recovery.

It had been an unusually snowy winter in southwest Wisconsin. Checking the forecast, there was a measureable amount forecasted for the weekend, but just a few inches. Nevertheless, I was looking at a three-and-a-half hour drive and didn't look forward to getting caught anywhere along my route, especially with my favorite feline patient. He was safe and secure in the cat carrier that was strapped in the seat belt. Several years earlier I had knit an afghan using up the last of many colorful skeins of yarn to create a large and heavy covering that was now doubled and wrapped around the carrier. My car gave off adequate heat but I wanted to make sure Sebastian was warm and comfortable. He would still be healing from his surgeries and I wanted to take every precaution. After all, it was January and the air was particularly brisk.

With a hug and a wave to Dad, we pulled out of the garage and headed down the road. It was about 3:30 PM and I wanted to be well on my way before it got too dark.

As we were pulling out of town it had begun to flurry and as we got going on the highway south to Cuba City, the flurries were accumulating and creating snow-covered patches that gave a jagged effect to the roadway. I was sure to slow down trying to stay in control. My apprehension and anxiety rose as I wondered what the rest of our journey would hold.

As we finished the first nine miles of our trip and came into the outskirts of Cuba City, I questioned myself about whether to turn back or continue the trip.

Glancing at the fuel gauge, it registered a little over a half tank. I pulled into my usual fuel station and needed to ask someone for an updated, real time road report. On the other side of the gas pump island, an older gentleman fueled his pickup truck. He could have been a farmer in his blue jeans, t-shirt and long sleeved flannel shirt. I hoped he could give me some insight. I secured the fuel hose and pushed the regular unleaded button and took a few steps in his direction.

"Excuse me. I'm driving to Chicago, do you happen to know

how safe the roads are?" I nervously inquired.

"Oh sure! They're in good shape and passable." He said with firm conviction.

"Oh really? The road from Platteville was patchy with blowing snow. It was drifting in spots. I'm a little nervous." I pressed on for more affirmation.

"Oh, you'll be okay. I just retired from the highway department after thirty years and you should be fine."

Well, there you have it. God placed just the right person at the right time to calm my fears. And what better representative than someone who kept a watchful eye over the road conditions for some thirty years? Breathing a heavy sigh and relaxing my muscles, I collected my receipt and continued onto Benton, Shullsburg, and then on to Gratiot. The roads didn't seem to be all that bad.

However, coming out of Gratiot the snow had accumulated and began to blow and drift again. The plows hadn't been out yet and if they had, the blowing quickly covered the roadway. About five miles out, I was cautiously approaching the downward slope of the snow covered two lane road with three pickups making their way towards me. The size, weight and construction of their vehicles made it easy for them to navigate the road conditions. They were no match for my little Ford Escort and I applied pressure to the brakes again trying to exercise control through the snow. As I tried to carefully guide my vehicle down the hill, the car began to slide as the wheels discovered an icy surface underneath the snow. Within moments I successfully managed to continue sliding ever so slowly about eight to ten feet off the road plowing and wedging the front wheels into several inches of snow.

Now I'd experienced numerous Wisconsin winters and knew if I could rock my car back-and-forth from 'drive' to 'reverse' that maybe, just maybe, I could establish a path and manage to get myself out and back on my way.

Are you kidding? That technique only served to further entrench my car into this almost now solid wall of snow. I was—STUCK! Period. Paragraph.

You remember those three pickup trucks? (Were they angels in disguise?) One stopped and checked with the pickup that just happened to be following me. It was decided that the gentlemen following me would drive me back into town until a tow could be arranged. A phone call to the local towing outfit proved fruitless as they were already on a call and had another activity going on that evening and couldn't make it. Keep in mind the advancing weather conditions and this was outside of a little burg; a very small burg where there are other priorities. My car would have to 'camp out' overnight off the road and surrounded by snow covered cornfields. We would have to get back into Gratiot and stay the night.

I grabbed the afghan covered carrier and with the carrier on my lap, Sebastian and I rode into town in this pickup. The gentlemen at the wheel seemed like the grandfatherly type and we had a nice conversation going into town which didn't take that long. He was able to navigate the snow covered roadway very well. Thank heavens!

There's only one hotel in the small town of Gratiot (population 216) and I'd driven past it many, many times on my way to Platteville and back. It was a large nondescript rectangular building. Nothing fancy. Two entrances; one for the bar and one for the restaurant. On some weekends during the summer months there would be someone dressed up as a yellow chicken, prancing back and forth with a sign advertising their wonderful chicken. Some weekends the weather was quite warm. I just hoped whoever the lucky person was, they paid him well. During the hunting and snowmobiling seasons, the hotel was kept pretty busy with those needing a bed, a good, hot, home-cooked meal and a beer or two.

On this particular night there was a local firemen's party scheduled so there would be activity and noise in the house. I didn't care. We just needed a place to crash. I mean, bed down for the night.

It was still light out when we arrived and climbed up the cement steps into the bar area. The gentleman who drove us there began explaining our predicament to the barkeep, "This young lady needs a room for the night. Her car is stuck in the snow about five miles south of town and the tow truck can't make it out tonight."

The tall, grey haired man behind the bar who had seen many a late night and whose thin shoulders kept up his suspenders leaned into the bar with both outstretched arms and replied, "Yeah, we've got a room for ya."

"How much is the room?" I inquired.

"Fifteen bucks!"

"Okay." I was quite surprised and pleased but wondered what sort of a room we would end up with for the night.

"There's a restaurant on the other side that serves up a pretty good meal. Tonight's the firemen's party so it'll be lively," he added. He could have been the owner, I didn't know for sure. I handed him my fifteen bucks.

"I've got my cat with me," I added and took off the afghan revealing Sebastian to the gentlemen.

"Oh, a little kitty," he remarked as his demeanor perked up. For a second he didn't seem to be the rough and tumble bouncer type. And then it was back to business.

"Here's the key. It's the room to the right down the hall. The washroom's at the end of the hall."

"Thank you," I said gratefully.

And then I turned to our chauffeur... "Thank you so much for driving us into town." I told the gentlemen who helped us.

"I'll be back tomorrow around 9:00 o'clock to pick you up and meet the tow truck," he responded.

"Ok. Sounds good. See you then. Thanks again." I was very thankful for his help and availability.

As he turned and left the bar, I grabbed the carrier with Sebastian in it and found the door that separated the bar from the restaurant. The opened door revealed a set of well-worn steps that creaked and cracked as we made our way up through the dark, narrow stairway. There was a light at the top of the stairs. I found our room and braced as I reminded myself of how much I paid for it. Turning the key and opening the door, I flipped on the light and in the dim there was a narow room long enough to accommodate a single bed in front of a window, an end table next to the bed with a dated lamp and another small, square table at the bottom of the bed and a futon. On the smaller, square table was an 8" black-and-white TV. There was nothing fresh about the furnishings and the air was a little stale but it was for one night and it would have to do.

After settling in and setting up Sebastian's oatmeal litter box, food and water station, I went back downstairs and enjoyed a wonderful chicken dinner. The restaurant was doing a brisk business by this time. After my meal I could have stayed and had a drink at the bar, maybe even met some of the clientele, but decided I should spend time with Sebastian. He needed comforting and I hoped he would forgive me after his surgery. We also needed to bond. I turned on the TV and Sebastian and I watched and listened to those melodic old tunes on the Lawrence Welk Show.

I called my brother and a few friends to let them know of our location and situation. All I could do was laugh at our predicament. I mean, here we were out in the middle of nowhere, snowed in at this little hotel with a little black-and-white TV and watching none other than Lawrence Welk. Watching the program brought back lots of memories when we lived at the 'old' house just next door to the one Dad built, the house we eventually moved in to. Saturday nights back then was 'bath night.' After we four had taken our baths and dressed in our pajamas and robes, besides Lawrence Welk, we'd furnish the entertainment for Dad and Mother. We'd try our best to dance in step to the rhythm of the music and took great delight in their laughter at our comical attempts. Mother, in particular, had a low threshold for entertainment and laughter.

"Why didn't you call me? I would have come pull you out." my brother scolded.

"But Gary, it was near blizzard conditions and by the time you would have gotten here you would have gotten stuck, too. We're fine, we're warm and there'll be a tow truck to pull us out tomorrow. We're safe for tonight. Don't worry, ok?" I explained in defense. And we

February, 2009, about five miles south of Gratiot, Wisconsin. You can see the hook up of the tow truck behind the back wheel as it was about to be pulled out of the snow. As you can see by the snow around the front tire, we weren't going anywhere on our own.

were warm. Sebastian had food and water. And the bathroom was clean and quite adequate for my needs for the night.

It wasn't long and the loud hum of the motors on the snowmobiles broke the silence of the cold night. I looked out the window and down at the black snowsuits dismounting the machines as they removed their gloves and adjusted their visors while deciding what their next moves would be; to come in and enjoy a meal, a drink or just continue on their way and make the most of the fresh snowfall.

Alas, they decided to continue on their trek through the snowy terrain and make the most of the evening despite the cold. It had stopped snowing by now so conditions were perfect.

The noise from the party downstairs, and the occupant's activities next door well into the early morning hours, made for a short night with only a quick nap. After a little freshening up in the washroom, Sebastian and I were ready to meet the day. I gathered our belongings and we made our way downstairs to the bar. The same barkeep from the night before stood behind the bar and upon seeing us, summoned the pickup truck driver who drove us the night before. The addition of darkened circles under his eyes proved that he, too, was just a tad weary from his short night. He placed another call to the towing out-fit. Soon, Sebastian and I were on our way to my buried car.

It was Sunday morning and the sky was blue as can be. The air was cold and crisp and the sun shone brightly reflecting off of the snow crystals that flocked most everything in sight. We met the tow truck driver who invited us to stay in his cab while he unleashed the chains to be hooked onto my car. The rattling of the chains and the loud motor made an alarming noise and Sebastian was frantic with anxiety as I allowed him to check out the dashboard of the cab. I grabbed hold of him and held him close to me wrapping the afghan around him. I read somewhere that cats enjoy being sung to so I be-gan humming some aimless tune that seemed to calm him down. This would be quite an adventure that would further bond Sebastian and I.

In a few hours we would be home, safe and warm.

Sebastian and Me
A Confrontation

*Cats' hearing apparatus is built to allow
the human voice to easily go in one ear
and out the other.*

Stephen Baker

It was Monday morning and I had errands to run. As I gathered
my belongings near the door, Sebastian became more anxious and
agitated at the realization that I would be leaving him alone—again!
He picked up on my intentions earlier as he heard the water running in
the shower. He knew what was coming—or going in this case.

He scampered toward the door abruptly braking at the opening
meowing his plea to go with me!

"No!" I firmly announced.

"Meeeoooooow," he countered me.

No!" I affirmed. Yet another "meeoow." I could see this was not
going to be an easy departure.

"No, you can't go this time." Sebastian stepped away from the
door and we locked gazes.

"Meeeooooow." He sorrowfully pleaded on having his way.

"No!" I bent over and met his stare and with yet another stern
directive, "No, you can't come with me this time."

Sebastian knew what "No" meant but insisted on trying to change
my mind. It wasn't often I relented.

We had departed together at times, down the hall, the stairs and
on out the door for a nice frolic in the woods just north of us. There
was no need for a leash. He would follow me and together we would
trek along the walking path through the wooded area and around the
pond. But not today.

23

I dressed, put on the finishing touches, picked up my things and slowly approached the door with him at my heels all the while repeating, "No, you can't go."

As I carefully and slowly opened the door, I used my bag and purse as a barrier to keep him back but he found an opportunity and raced out the door sprinting several feet ahead of me. He had achieved his goal! He was 'free!' But, as if on a leash, he knew it was to be short lived. The look on his whiskered little face told the whole story, "Let's see how far I can go with my escape," he thought tenaciously.

We lived on the second floor and with one eye on the stairs going down and one eye on me, he slowly descended the first three steps, and turned around to see me drop my bags waiting for his adventure to end. He knew it was coming. He just wanted to exercise his defiance.

Sebastian turned and once again began descending the stairs to the bottom and went around the corner, oh so quietly, so as to not disturb the other residents, as if that were possible with his thick, soft paws. I stood at the top of the stairs and angrily whispered loudly, "Sebastian, GET BACK HERE!"

A moment later there appeared a whisker, then an ear and finally, the eye. He was being so coy. After another plea for him to return, he knew he had better surrender and slowly began ascending the stairs. Once he arrived at the top he crossed the hallway and as if in slow motion began descending the opposite stairs.

Again, after creeping down the first three steps, and hoping I would change my mind yet again, I assured him he needed to get back up the stairs. I leaned over and beckoned to him, but he turned and continued his trek down the stairs settling near the door looking up at me waiting for further instruction. 'My intention is to go OUTside, Mom!' With one hand on my hip and the other visibly pointing to the floor, I sternly advised him to, "Get Up Here—NOW!"

Finally, he surrendered and slowly came up the stairs. Or so I thought. He walked right past me and started down the hallway in the opposite direction again. Oh, so clever. I felt as though I were fish-

He could really try my patience.

ing and just about had my catch of the day. He was really trying my patience.

Something triggered his sniffer into action and he crouched along the floorboard. I gave him a few more moments and then carefully came up behind him, picked him up ever so gently and carried him back to our apartment. I held him in a loving embrace assuring him that even though I had to leave for the day, I still loved him. He didn't fight it.

He absorbed my soothing tone of voice and surrendered. I wanted him to know I wasn't punishing him. Opening the jarred door, I gently put him down, and he scampered back in to our living space accepting his plight. I won this one. "I'm the one in charge here." I thought to myself. What a deception.

This scenario was only one incident of many, as this was repeated often whenever I had to leave the apartment. I learned that if I allowed him out in the hall by even leading him there as if in giving him permission, that when I had to leave without him, my departures got easier. With a firm 'no,' he would turn around and walk several feet away from the door inside the apartment understanding that he really couldn't go with me. And there would be another opportunity when he would be able to leave. I was pleased when he understood and respected my wishes. I would tell him what a 'good boy' he was. But then, he is a cat.

Sebastian on the Patio

Now you See me—Now you Don't

> *Dogs come when they are called,*
> *Cats take a message and get back to you later.*
> **Mary Bly**

Feral cats aren't wild. They just love their freedom. We live on the second floor with a sliding glass door going out to a small patio. The unit is a 90 degree angle from the next closest neighbors and with two large trees in front we're rather secluded. With me being a 'free spirit' myself, I could identify and sympathize with Sebastian's true nature and lust for adventure. From time to time when the weather permitted, I would allow him out on the patio to check out the grounds below and what he could see going on in the back parking lot. For some time now he seemed to be content just peering through the railing.

Cats love to be on a higher surface so they can view the scenery beneath them. It's part of their nature. Maybe they get a sense of empowerment from it. At any rate he loved to lie down, stretch out and sun himself. And he loved the fresh air, the birds tweeting in the trees and the warmth and independence that the outing provided him. In the Spring when the blackbirds would be nesting above the door in the dryer vent, there would be quite a bit of chatter going on when Sebastian was out there. Papa blackbird would be scolding and raising such a raucous protecting the brood he wanted to attend to. Mama blackbird was none too happy about Sebastian's presence either. When he was bored or ready to come in, he'd 'meow' his request and I'd slide the door back and he would once again happily take up residence on the couch, curl up and take yet another nap.

However, one day I let him out and closed the door as usual but then had some errands to run. I was in my car, about to pull out but forgot my cell phone. When I went back upstairs, I grabbed my phone but stopped short. Where was Sebastian? Usually he would have been right at the door at the sound of the turning of the key. But this time he wasn't at the door. Where did I leave him last? Check the patio. "Sebastian!" Oh my gosh. He could have been out there for hours, I thought. I let him in quickly, said a 'thank you' prayer to my angels and was on my way again.

Whenever I let him out onto the patio I would check on him every once in a while just to satisfy my curiosity. But there was this other occasion he wasn't there—! I went out on the deck and looked down to see him looking up at me as if to say, "Look what I did, Ma!"

Alarmed at the sight, I quickly pivoted, grabbed my keys and went down the stairs and outside to retrieve him. He wasn't too eager to be captured and brought back home. He gave me quite a chase before he finally surrendered. Apparently his curiosity got the better of him.

I discovered he would use the lilac bush just off the right of the deck to break his fall. How he managed to not harm himself, again was an intervention of the angels. The bush was heavy with leaves to soften the fall. I was just thankful he didn't end up with a branch piercing his body. He was really pushing the envelope as this occurred more than once much to my consternation. I felt that with each attempt of trying to achieve his freedom that there was that possibility of one day he just may not come back! What a frightening thought knowing how adventurous and anxious he was to explore whatever horizons were out there. He jumped down a few more times before he decided that wasn't the route he wanted to take and stayed on the patio.

Here's Sebastian eyeing a blackbird who wants to tend to his/her babies. One day Sebastian was on the patio one moment and the next he was gone. Summer of 2009.

The Animal Control Van
I'm in Trouble Now

*My cat is an angel from heaven with
sandpaper kisses and a heart full of love*

I let Sebastian outside on this one particular summer day through the front door of the building. He had so much energy and after a short romp, I called for him to come back, but he didn't return. "Sebaaaaaaastiiiian, where arrrrre you?"

After checking with several neighbors who were within sight, I found myself in the middle of the parking lot and carefully scanned my surroundings for my four legged, orange-colored friend. I took a few extra moments and came up with nothing.

It was then that I noticed a white van, with the words, 'McHenry County Animal Control,' come around the drive and continue beyond the garages before ending up in the lot of the next building behind the dumpsters. Now, I thought, "what would be the chances that someone found him, kept him long enough to make a call and this was the van they were waiting for." Call it intuition, a gut feeling, my sixth sense, whatever, but I was motivated to find out. Sure enough, about five parking slots in and in front of the neighboring building, there was the van. I saw the uniformed man get out of his van with a clipboard in hand and enter the building. What timing!

I waited a few moments and then went back to my original location. Within a few short minutes the van driver came around the corner, saw me out in the middle of the lot, turned into the lot and parked in front of me. His window was already down on the passenger side.

"Are you missing a cat?" he bent forward over the steering wheel and asked.

"Yes." I answered rather sheepishly. Now how did he know I was the one missing a cat? Maybe because I was standing in the middle of the parking lot appearing rather lost myself? Makes sense.

He got out of his truck, came around the side door, unlatched and slid the door open revealing a rather large cage with none other than my little Sebastian inside. He appeared a little shell-shocked and "bus-ted!" Big time!

"He may be a little wet because of the bowl of water in here." The driver offered his explanation. He seemed to be very kind.

"How much do I owe you?" I was reluctant to ask him but felt I had to. I was surely relieved to see this little guy. Again, my angels (and his angel) were on duty.

"With this being a holiday, I would ordinarily charge $75 (it was Labor Day), but I'll waive it this time. Just keep your pet indoors." He advised. How lucky could I be? If that wasn't divine intervention; thank you, Angels!

He was very nice and polite about his mission and ordeal. This was no doubt just routine for him. And yet another adventure for my little Sebastian!

Now this little snippet in the life and fun times with Sebastian may sound a little hokey but this is exactly how it played out. Remember, there are no accidents and angels are constantly working on our behalf. They were surely with us that day. Once again, Sebastian was back home. Sigh!

Sebastian Walks Away

"Gone...!"

"Sebastian's Rite of Passage"

You don't own a cat.
The best you can do is be partners

Sir Henry Swanson

"I don't know how you can let him out like that!" my friend exclaimed and scolded in the middle of our conversation. Sebastian, my cat, had disappeared three days earlier. We were at her home and she was seated with her back leaning against the arm of the couch, her legs outstretched on the cushions. One arm was resting on the back of the couch while the other in her lap.

"Well, I'm learning my lesson this time." I confessed. I was seated and slumped on the other couch in her living room feeling extremely guilty and abandoned. I reflected on how it all began...

*   *   *

It was Saturday morning, November 7th. I was meeting a girlfriend for breakfast, playing 'beat the clock' as usual. Within a short time, Sebastian picked up on it and quickly voiced his bid to escape the confines of our apartment. Sebastian was about a year and a half old and full of energy and curiosity. The temperature outside was creeping up into the 60's with a warm wind and bright sunshiny skies. Now how could I deny him the adventure on this absolutely beautiful day? I was running out of time. Grabbing my purse and keys, I headed for the door of our apartment unit with Sebastian quickly overcoming me and waiting at the door. I remember it well.

"Ok, fella. You'd better be good!" And together we made our way out into the beautiful sunshine. When I returned later that afternoon, Sebastian hadn't. This scenario wasn't all that unusual. Since the weather was still unseasonably warm and breezy, I wasn't too concerned as he had stayed out all night before…a couple of times! Sunday's weather was a carbon copy of Saturday's, but then that evening, Sebastian still hadn't returned. We'd been together a little over a year and I thought he would have become pretty familiar with his surroundings but now I was becoming anxious and my mind began to race creating all sorts of possibilities. Had he met his fate with a critter from the preserve just north of us? Had he walked into the path of a moving car? We lived among several close knit buildings and garages. Maybe he was cat napped! He was so cute.

As I followed the walking path around the complex I saw a pipe in a ravine. Could he be stuck in that pipe or any other trying to seek shelter? Had someone taken him in and decided they could take better care of him than I? Or, had he just wandered off and was, indeed, seriously 'lost?' There were all kinds of possibilities.

By Sunday afternoon, I began a more serious search for my little lost feline. As I walked the sidewalks around the buildings nearby, I checked the bushes and any other hiding places or behind any corners where he might have been crouching. No Sebastian. After a little breakfast the following morning, dressed in my warm, heavy, hooded sweatshirt and baseball cap, I took off toward the park just north of the apartment trekking through some of the well-worn paths he and I had hiked on. The warm weather held steadfast, fall leaves crunched under my steps as I called out his name every few feet. The silence was deafening.

Later that afternoon, I ventured out around the other apartment units, up and down the sidewalks searching and stopping only to peer into the thick evergreens that crowded around the entrances whispering loudly, "Sebastian! Are you in there?" No rustling of the branches, no tail swishing, no pair of eyes peering out through the branches. Not even a whisker.

My anxiety was mounting as I tried to get into the head of my wanderer, tracing some of our steps on our walks. Enough time had passed that he could have wandered quite a distance, so I got into my car and slowly traveled the subdivisions surrounding the complex where we lived, crossing main streets and hoping to find the flick of his tail darting out from behind a bush or sauntering in between the single family homes. Would he be so brave as to cross a street away from the buildings in the complex? There were so many hiding places in our midst. From our walks to the park, wasn't he satisfied to stay within those perimeters?

After some Internet research I learned that more often than not, they stick relatively close to home. That gave me some momentary relief. Several friends had been alerted and placed us on their prayer lists. I know there's a specific angel assigned to watch over lost things and especially animals. I wasn't sure but thought it to be St. Francis.

I would stop every few moments hoping for some movement among the leaves, but alas, nothing stirred among the foliage. Only the branches on the trees waving in the breeze as if to remind me, 'too bad, so sad, your kitty's gone away and you're slowly going mad.' Very funny.

There was a parking lot near a horse stable where several horses were out enjoying the beautiful fall day in their corral. They turned to acknowledge me and wondered why I had come to interrupt their day.

"Hi fellas! Just looking for my cat." I thought they should know my intentions.

"Hey! Have you... seen him?" I asked lamely. Of course, I was wasting my time. Silly. I sighed as I shook my head.

Beyond the parking lot was a path that led down to a small park with a pond that was graced with a picnic gazebo. Off to the right was a small gathering of geese exchanging news of the day. The path was paved and inviting as I started out my hike enjoying the scenery and wound my way around the pond. About midway through I discovered a cement walkway under the well-traveled road overhead and walked through it wondering if Sebastian's curiosity would take him this far away from the apartment. There was no sign of him, so I turned and headed back toward the car. It was still light out. I was hoping he wouldn't wander this far away. It was contrary to my research anyway.

When I returned back home, I e-mailed my friends to let them know of Sebastian's status. Many were concerned as I had alerted them earlier and asked for continued prayers for his safe return. Some would offer suggestions of places to look for him; stop at the local police station and report him missing, check the area shelters. What about the Humane Society or Animal Control places, besides making up flyers and posting them inside the entrances of the other buildings in the complex? Then I posted a photo with my phone number on it in a grocery store nearby. I picked out a few photos and copied them along with my 'Lost and Found' notation. I found out I could place a free ad in the local paper. But that would only be good for a week. And then I went around the immediate neighborhood several times a day looking for him and posted my 'Lost' sign in the front foyers of the numerous buildings. With me being out of work, I had the time to do these things. And too much time to worry and fret.

I checked the Internet, and under 'Lost Pets,' I read that an orange tabby had been turned in at an animal control facility just north of here by a few miles. I was so excited! I mean how many 'orange tab-bies' can there be that came up missing, right? I loaded his carrier and a small bag of food in the car, and made sure I had my purse with me as I was almost sure there would be a charge.

I pulled into the parking lot of the animal control building that next morning. Inside I was greeted by one of the attendants who took me back down a hall and into one of the 'holding rooms' where I was shown at least a dozen lonely cats of all sizes, colors and breeds. One particularly young, gray, tabby reached out his paw and wanted me to take him home in the worst way. I quickly scanned the cages only to discover Sebastian was not among them. Sigh.

The attendant took me to yet another room of cats and kittens want-ing to go home with someone, anyone. Some were just bemused and not sure what was happening. There was one large, fat, grey one that actu-ally growled at me! I could see he wasn't going home to anyone anytime soon. Again, Sebastian was not among them. My hopes were dashed!

My heart sank as I stood at the counter, slowly and sadly giving the description of my dearly missed little companion. I was so disappointed.

"I have a photo of him." I quickly offered as I gave a picture of Sebastian to the clerk behind the desk. Surely this photo would bring him home.

"Oh, this is good. If we hear of anything we'll notify you." She assured me.

"Thank you." I said glumly as I turned to leave and go back home, —Cat-less.

On the way home, I began to think of my own life and how, within the last two years, I had lost or let go of so much already. I had walked out of nearly ten years of an unhealthy union with my husband. I left the beautiful new home I had always wanted; dreamed of. The fireplace we both fell in love with. The huge walk-in closet in the master bedroom I could nearly place a couch and overstuffed chair in. I'd always had just one small closet and now with the two bedrooms besides ours, I was blessed with three large closets! We had just poured a beautiful cement patio out back to accommodate our new hot tub, too! I was hoping I could turn things around.

However, the love and respect that was to be the glue that would keep us together had not been given the proper nourishment, attention or devotion. I sought the refuge of sanity from that environment and escaped. Now I was free! Free to make my own decisions. Free to satisfy my hunger for life. Free to meet my own needs and not depend on someone else's whims, judgments or limitations. And then, several months after having been on my own, I found myself without a job; a victim of a plunging housing market. With nothing tying me down, now I could run away, too. Sebastian kept me grounded. Sane. Responsible. Needed. And loved.

A few months earlier, as I was reading through the want ads in the local library, there appeared not one, not two, but three ads for "Free Kittens!" After the second phone call, I connected with a nice lady who had several available. And so began my relationship with this wonderful orange tabby that would be named Sebastian.

I needed a companion who would love unconditionally. He didn't care if there were dishes in the sink; if the laundry wasn't done, if the bed was left unmade. All he wanted was a warm place to stay, be fed, watered, petted and loved. Bingo! A Heavenly-sent Band-Aid. And he was such a beautiful animal with tabby markings and what seemed an extraordinarily long, striped tail. I was most taken by his large emerald green eyes. It wasn't long and we were fast friends He learned some of my habits and I picked up on some of his needs.

It was a very comfortable and satisfying union that was not only healthy but healing, too. I thanked God more than once for creating such a beautiful animal and companion. One of the main reasons why we bonded and created a high level of attachment was for one, I was single and two, I was the main person taking care of him. Together we created several rituals that formed our bond.

One ritual being when I got up in the night, he did too, and beckoned for me to accompany him to his feeding dish, which was in the second bathroom. Half asleep, I would reluctantly follow and sit on the commode while he partook of his "midnight snack," glancing up now and again to make sure I would remain until he was satisfied. A long, healthy stretch and he was ready to play for a few minutes. I had bought him a long, nylon tube where he would be on one end and I would peer at him through the other. Then, in what seemed to be a split second in the darkened room, he would bolt through and scare the b'jeebers out of me. Then we would return to the foot of my bed where we would take up where we left off, drifting into a peaceful slumber.

Now my question was, "Didn't he miss those moments together?" My heart ached at his absence. I didn't miss my ex-husband, but I surely missed my little companion! Did his disappearance mean that I was healed and didn't need a companion? Did he feel as though he was no longer needed? They can be so independent. Do they really care? I didn't know if these thoughts entered their being. Would he remember where he lived as dogs do? Their owners can move while the animal is missing and still find the owners through their scent senses. None the less, had my neglect prompted this latest escapade? Was this

He may have traveled this path on his trek to who knows where...

a mirror of my own now defunct marriage? It certainly gave me cause to pause and debate no matter how far-fetched it seemed.

Maybe this was God's way of communicating with me. I had really grown to love and depend on Sebastian's unconditional love. Is God a jealous God who wanted all of my attentions and loyalty?

Maybe this was His way of reminding me where my priorities should be. If I'd given God the honor and daily consult I should have in the first place, I may not have been in this situation now. Maybe this was His way of teaching me lessons I needed to learn.

He gives us Free Will to make our own decisions and choices. We can be so hapless sometimes and tend to lose our way. But eventually, if we listen to our hearts and angel whispers, God speaks words of comfort and direction (that still, small voice inside) and brings us back to Him. Would he return Sebastian to me? Or at least keep him safe from the elements? Questions. I had so many questions.

> *Be anxious for nothing, but in everything by*
> *prayer and supplication with thanksgiving let*
> *your requests be made known to God.*

Philippians 4:6 (NAS)

Sebastian was one of God's own little creatures; unconditional love incarnate; but he was now free to make his own decisions. Free to satisfy his hunger for life and all the adventure that was out there. He didn't have to depend on me to meet his needs. He could come and go as he pleased. No more closed doors. He was free! There was no commitment on his part to stay. I had to pray and trust God to bring him back safely. I was grateful my friends were doing the same. There's power in prayer. And I believed in the power of prayer.

Did Sebastian have lessons to learn that he could only learn away from the comforts and confines of home? There was such a parallel and learning curve going on between the two of us it was uncanny. If God was trying to get through to me, He surely knew how to speak to my heart and soul. And then there was a break. This was the ad that was printed up in the 'Lost Pets' column through the local newspaper and thankfully ran indefinitely.

> Lost: Orange tabby cat, white bib, male, neutered, front declawed. Answers to the name of Sebastian. Last seen Nov. 7, in _____ apartment complex, Lake in the Hills. Please call 123-456-7890.

A Break in the Saga
A phone call...

Of all animals, the cat alone attains
to the contemplative life.

Andrew Lang

It was over a week since his disappearance and I was on my way to the animal shelter where I had been almost a week earlier with his carrier certain that, according to the shelter's web site, yet another orange tabby had just been brought in. I recalled a lady friend who, the day before, had advised I pray to St. Francis, the patron saint of lost animals so it was confirmed. One of the people whom I had met during my sojourn was a friendly fellow named, 'Josh.' Josh and his bicycle riding buddies had helped me round up Sebastian a time or two before and he seemed to be a very kind and gentle young man about eleven or twelve years old. He was talkative, sensitive and most helpful.

"Oh St. Francis, please bring Sebastian home safely." I pleaded as I made my way to the shelter. I hadn't reached the shelter yet, when my cell phone rang.

"Hi! This is Josh," the young voice said…"and I just saw your cat!" Josh wouldn't lead me astray.

As soon as I could I turned the car around and headed back home. Josh lived in the same complex and in the building just south of us. He knew how much Sebastian meant to me. He had grown to care for him, too.

"Are you home?" I questioned in haste.

"Yes, did you want me to wait outside?" Josh said.

"Oh, if it's not too cold. I'll be there shortly." I was maybe five, ten minutes away.

"Ok, I can do that." He cheerfully answered.

In cruising the different apartment building parking lots, Josh had come up to the car and informed me that he had seen Sebastian before in the neighborhood and would be happy to catch him for me. And on this day his voice sounded as pleased and as excited as I was to hear the news.

Once back in the parking lot where Josh said he had seen him, I hurriedly parked my car to see Josh approach me on his bike. Of course, Sebastian had disappeared out of sight by now. At least I now knew that he was 1) Alive and well. And 2) In the vicinity. What a tremendous relief that was. For the next forty-five minutes, Josh, his mother, sister and I walked around the complex in search of my little, elusive four-legged friend. But to no avail. They were being so helpful.

Now I could at least notify my contingent of prayers that they could relax as he had been spotted and there was hope. Up until that point, I had been told of how Sebastian could have become some animal's meal, and that some people still consume cats. I couldn't imagine the absolute horror of such a thing and wondered about the person who would even inform me of such behaviors. Apparently they thought I needed to be aware of this or were they just exercising their knowledge? I wasn't impressed. And then I heard that one particular individual had actually gassed cats that came into his yard for disrupting the vegetation! I didn't need to hear that either. Or did I?

I sensed Sebastian was a 'free spirit' also. It came natural to him. The cup of my stress level was overflowing. All of these observations had been part of the tape that began to replay itself in my head after having been out searching for hours and it was just about more than I could take. I wasn't eating properly and would search at different times of the day; early in the morning, mid-morning, late afternoon, late at night.

One particular evening I was following the paved walking path headed for the pond with a flashlight. A few steps into my search and I heard a rustling in the weeds to my left. I aimed my flashlight and up on the hill the light reflected off of two eyes peering down at me with the silhouette of a rack of antlers. A deer! He stood so proud and regal. I really didn't venture any further and returned home. One good thing to come out of all of this was the exercise. It helped with my weight loss. And there was plenty of fresh air. It was still November.

DAY 8 AND 9: the days came and went as I continued my search and possible rescue of my little, furry buddy. The memories of our time together would surface one by one as I recalled an evening when Sebastian appeared to be bored. Case in point…

I thought I would be his playmate for a while. An article I read advised ten minutes of play a day for bonding. So, one evening, getting down on all fours, I slowly crept around the love seat in the living room. I knew he was on the other end. Half way around, I thought I'd check his location. Lowering my head to the floor and peering under the couch, I found two large eyes staring back at me. I couldn't help but do a 'tuck and roll' over in spontaneous laughter as I foolishly thought I was going to pull a fast one on him. Who was I kidding? Upon gathering my wits, I continued around until I got near the end and all of a sudden Sebastian jumped out at me. It was only a moment in time, but I remembered it with such delight and warmth.

It was the early afternoon of DAY 11 and I was on my routine trek checking the different building parking lots. I saw an older resident had just returned home from grocery shopping. As the lady emptied her car trunk of the bags, I slowly approached her and asked if she had seen an orange tabby cat.

"Yes! I've seen him walk across my patio several times."

"Oh really?" I exclaimed. Holy moly! I couldn't believe it. Another sighting! And he was still alive!

"Sometimes he'll walk behind the garages there and go back along the buildings." She added.

"Oh, thank you!" I sighed with relief with my hand on my chest. "If you see him again, would you please call me? I'll be here as soon as I can!"

"Oh surely!"

She went on to explain how she, herself, was soon to become a cat owner and knew how special they can be. I reminded her of the sign I had posted inside the entryway with my cell number. A cat would be great company for her.

Day 11 and my cell phone rang once again. Someone had seen an orange and white tabby cat along a heavily traveled road just north of me, had seen my ad in the paper and thought to alert me of their finding. After some discussion as to the description and exact location, we came to the conclusion that it wasn't Sebastian. The only white markings he had were under his neck and it was a small patch. The caller admitted to not wanting to make the call as the cat had apparently been hit and thrown, meeting his death at the hands of a speeding motorist. I was much relieved at this news and at the same time grateful for her observation.

Day 12: November 19th the car Sebastian had been comfortable riding in was soon to be replaced as it had met its demise in a freak accident that deemed it a "total loss." Now when I would travel through the neighborhoods, he wouldn't recognize me right away. My sister had lived about five minutes from the scene of the accident and was there to make sure I got home ok. I then divulged of Sebastian's absence.

"I didn't know that." She quietly replied. As if life had handed me yet another punch. I hadn't wanted to own up to my negligence in this recent escapade. She, herself had been a long time dog owner and was familiar with the affection and bond that is formed between an animal and human. At this point, she had already lost one dog and later two to old age. She was single, also.

The day before Thanksgiving I received yet another call from an excited older woman who confessed to feeding an orange tabby for the past three weeks. However, this cat had not been neutered or declawed which, again, canceled out Sebastian. He was still M.I.A.

Thanksgiving Day! I was up in Platteville, Wisconsin, driving in a cute little Nissan Sentra that I'd rented until I made the decision to replace my car. Dad was home after having spent time at the local nursing home. I helped him get dressed slipping on his shoes and tying

Barbara Key Park: This was a familiar path for both of us and we'd often see a bunny rabbit along the path. Sebastian would crouch down among the long blades of grass waiting for whatever came along the path. It was as if he were a lion in the jungle. "Hear me roar!"

them for him in readiness to meet the rest of the family at a popular restaurant just south of town. He really didn't want to go. He was tired and not feeling his best. This would be the last Thanksgiving we would have with him. Neither one of us acknowledged the fact but I think he was aware of it also and reluctantly joined the family.

In July, Dad had been diagnosed with multiple myeloma, a cancer of the blood plasma in the bone marrow, and after several radiation treatments and the excellent care he received at the nursing home, he was back home again.

Actually, Sebastian's absence was a blessing in disguise as he was not all that welcomed in the family. I really didn't need the stress of having to deal with those circumstances and seeing to his travel needs on top of Dad's poor health. Call it divine intervention. Again, I prayed that God and His angels were with dad and were looking out for Sebastian.

Can't Let Go

A Releasing of Faith?

All of us like sheep have gone astray.

Isaiah 53:6

DAY 21: Back in my apartment, and its 2:45 AM I'm awakened by a cat fight in the parking lot outside my bedroom window. Grabbing and wrestling with my housecoat I slipped on some shoes, and quickly made my way to the patio where I unlatched and slid the door open. The crisp night air was calm as I called out Sebastian's name in a loud whisper. In answer, I heard the mournful groan of an injured cat and then nothing. Not giving up on this latest bit of evidence, I grabbed my keys and launched down the stairs and outside into the cool, quiet din of early morning and again whispering loudly, "Se-baaaastian." And then I whistled into the darkness hoping to hear a response. Nothing. My intentions were met with nothing. No Sebastian. And no one. Sigh.

In reflection, how often has God called on us? How often have we not 'heard' that still, small voice calling out in our hearts? Have we been so preoccupied or 'lost' in our own thoughts, selfish desires, and needs to hear Him advising us trying to get our attention? Directing our paths? Leading us to make certain choices and decisions that would make all the difference in our lives?

Slowly I turned and started back into the building, turning one more time and scanning the lot for any sign of Sebastian. My silent pleas were futile

DAY 22: I've decided that he will come home on his own terms. Having heard of personal accounts from other cat owners on the return of their felines, the time element ranged from five to thirty days. And then years. I pampered myself with that thought and that Sebastian's return seemed more of a reality now and I could relax and just wait. There was new cat litter, plenty of food and less cat hair to contend with now that I vacuumed and made way for his presence once again! I even straightened up 'his' room! Now why wouldn't a spoiled cat want to come back home, I asked myself.

I could no longer justify the length of his 'vacation' and quietly accepted the fact that his appearance was eminent! Down-trodden and exhausted, I went to bed and slept soundly! I turned my dilemma over to Jesus, the saints and His angels and let them handle it.

DAY 24: I was in the middle of dressing for the day and my cell phone rang. This time the lady asked if I had found my cat. "No."

"I saw him over by the police station," she said she had called out his name and 'he' responded and then continued on his way toward this open field beyond the trees and brush. When he turned, he might not have recognized her, the voice, or the car and continued on his way.

"How soon can you be here?" She asked.

I told her in about 10 minutes. Absolutely elated, I stuffed a couple of Kleenexs in my pocket. I was going to finally see my Sebastian and was prepared to shed a tear or two. As I pulled up just past the police station I saw a woman dressed in a black snowmobile outfit, coming out of the woodsy area a short distance from the police station.

"Hi!" I anxiously yelled out to her and gave her a wave.

"Hi! I was driving by and saw this orange tabby. I see your sign posted in our building every day and called out, 'Sebastian!' Does he have white on his hind legs?"

"I really don't remember." At that moment, I honestly couldn't remember. Gosh, you'd think I'd know that. I was so excited that I was so close to finding my little feline.

"Thank you so much for calling me." I was so pleased that people were actually reading my notices in the buildings and responding. She must have been a pet owner herself.

"Ok, good luck." And she walked back to her car and drove off.

Before entering the open field, I had to pass through some tall brush that pulled at my slacks and sweatshirt. Dodging tree limbs, I called out, "Sebaaaastian…" and then whistled for him. I thought by now if he didn't acknowledge my voice, his memory may be triggered by the whistle. Stepping carefully through the bent weeds every few feet, I stopped and called out again, "Sebaaaastian…" Nothing. It was so quiet. December days can be like that.

Only the sound of an occasional chirp of a bird landing in a nearby tree or the rustle of the sheaves of beaten down vegetation was all that broke the silence. The ground was soft and murky in places and I had to watch my footing for puddles and mud. The skies overhead were overcast and appeared to be full of snowflakes that wanted to fall as the temperatures were hovering around the freezing mark. Time for Sebastian to come home. I thought in defiance and disgust.

Didn't he miss his 'blankie?' I would often spend time at my desk using the laptop in the office/his playroom. Exercising his curiosity and not wanting to be left alone in the other room he would soon follow and make himself comfortable in the corner rocking chair next to the desk. There he would settle himself curling up on the blanket I had spread out for him. On cue, I would fold over the sides one at a time covering him completely. He didn't seem to mind and slept peacefully for extended periods of time. Once in a while I would reach over and gently rub his back or fluff his fur to let him know I knew he was there and that he was loved. He hardly stirred and was content to be near his 'mom.' Such a great companion. And so loved. Wouldn't he miss this attention? The warmth? The lovin'?

Later that afternoon I drove around the same area and did see an orange tabby but with white legs. However, he was thicker than Sebastian so the jury was still out. My heart sank as I discovered 1) It wasn't him and 2) He had competition in this area and 3) I had to remind myself that I had had his front claws removed. A good thing for my furniture but a concern when he was out in the wild trying to defend himself. I later learned that they actually use their hind feet to defend themselves so I was feeling relieved about that fact. Nevertheless I felt

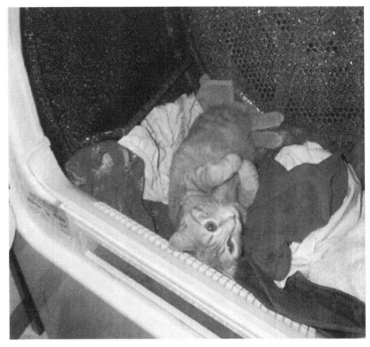

*What is it about dryers that are so attractive to our feline friends?
Maybe it's the heat and softness of the fabric besides another place to
'hide' in.*

uneasy about the whole thing.

Home once again; I glanced in the direction of his feeding dish,
which was still full of dry food. His litter box had been refreshed days
ago and his water bowl was empty awaiting a fresh supply when he
returned. The couch and love seat had been groomed with most of the
pet hair removed and the floors vacuumed. It appeared the prepara-
tions for his return were all set now.

He's a Feral Cat

What did I expect?

Feral: having returned to an untamed state from domestication
The American Heritage Dictionary

Christmas wrapping had begun and I would have thought he would want to jump back into his role of supervisor again this year, if not actually helping me wrap the packages as he had done before. He should have the procedure down pat, I thought, as he monitored my every move while crouching on the bar stool cushion in the corner of the room last year. So where was my little gift wrapping assistant this year?

It was DAY 26, December 3rd, and during this time of year, most everyone is 'preparing' for Christmas. People were making lists, checking them twice, baking, shopping, decorating their homes inside and out, getting ready for the most festive and colorful holiday with much anticipation.

And many, many years ago, three Wise Men journeyed many miles in search of the Christ child who would represent and bring Salvation to the masses all over the world. I felt a strange and maybe not so coincidental paradox here as I was 'journeying' through the woods and walking paths in search of my Little Road Warrior who had given me such pleasure, peace and healing for the past year! He was my tangible companion.

But God would always be in my heart and soul.

DAY 30: I was driving near the area where Sebastian was supposedly spotted near the police station and saw a black animal sitting near the edge of the woods as if it were stalking its prey. Stopping the car, I slowly approached and discovered it was a black, fat, cat with a white bib.

He only turned to acknowledge me and after a few minutes slowly made his way into the wooded area but only for a short distance. Now my thoughts turned to the possibility that he may have been in a scrape with something and was watching over the victim so I listened for any sign of life. An occasional rustle of the weeds kept me there for several minutes.

The sun was quickly exiting in the west so I went back to my car to retrieve my flashlight. Maybe I could catch a pair of green eyes reflecting back at me. Ok, so maybe that fat cat was just stalking some little varmint, which would be a relief. The chill in the wintry air was too much and after not hearing any groans of pain or activity, I decided to get a bite to eat. I wondered if I could eat at all. C'mon, how long can Sebastian stay out in this cold? Doesn't he miss his mama? We had exchanged lots of love and affection; was his wanderlust that overpowering? He was only a year and a half old.

It was plain to see that the answer to that question was a resounding "Yes!" He had been born on a farm and was considered a feral cat. This new lifestyle was what they were born to do. I came home and looked up 'feral cats' on my computer. There was a short video on their characteristics but I heard the narrator remark of how they were incredible survivors out in the wild. I hung on to that statement as I once again set out the next morning continuing my search.

DAY 31: I replayed the tape of the lady in the snowmobile suit who said he was skinny and after so long a period of time, that seemed to make sense. I wondered what his diet consisted of. I had hoped he still had his collar on. I had his name and my cell number engraved on the tag. If he had run into some folks who had taken him in I'd hope they would have called me by now.

When I open up my computer I will sometimes see an e-mail from a prominent veterinarian. He submits all kinds of information on cats and their needs. This morning I opened it up to read about how one can be a 'Responsible Cat Owner.' I read on with trepidation as I knew I would find myself listed there somewhere. Sure enough!

> POINT #7 Keep pets safe. Cats that are allowed to roam free are more commonly traumatized and victimized! Keep your Cat Safe.

BING-o! "Yes, your Honor," as I dropped my head and pled guilty to the above charges. "Go ahead, throw the book at me. I deserve it."

On my trek earlier that morning I saw several people out either accompanying their children to their appointed school bus stop or brushing off their cars from the night's snowfall. I caught the attention of a pretty lady who was dressed for work and asked if she had seen an "orange tabby cat."

"No, but I'll say a prayer for his return. I don't know how he would get to where he is going, but I will pray for him." I didn't quite understand that, but I appreciated her support. Ah! Someone who believed in miracles! She told me to pray to St. Anthony.

"No wonder! I've been bothering St. Francis!" I told her.

She went on to inform me that St. Anthony was the Saint for lost things. All righty then! St. Anthony it was!

"Thank you so much!" No wonder I wasn't seeing any results.

I was grateful for the information and 'told' St. Anthony to get off his duff as he had a mission to complete. All the while listening to a CD on "expecting the favor of God…"

As soon as I invited St. Anthony to join St. Francis, I began to turn it around and 'Thank' them for their help in locating and nudging Sebastian back to the home ranch. It's surprising what an Attitude of Gratitude can do for your spirit and feeling of expectation and hopefulness. It releases the endorphins that are so helpful in maintaining and extending one's life. Endorphins are our body's natural hormones that get released when we are doing something that requires a burst of energy. They also act as a pain relief when the body becomes too hurt to handle things. I wanted to believe all these things in the worst way.

> *All things are possible to him who believes.*
> **Mark 9:23**

DAY 31: afternoon. I needed to mail some things and pick up a few groceries. Yet another opportunity to spot my freedom loving feral kitty. I really didn't feel as though I could relax at this juncture as there was snow in the forecast but would be a forerunner of a nasty storm coming in starting the next evening and dumping several inches. Along with the snow would come some pretty cool temperatures and nasty winds creating drifts.

Again my anxiety level rose and I could feel the flight of my heart in my chest. Would these conditions be enough to drive him back home? I stopped myself short as I was reminded to release my faith and trust the angels and saints to direct Sebastian's path back to the front (or back) doors. I have a problem with that. I forget that there are other powers surrounding us that we do not see but are always working on our behalf. We just have to have faith, believe and trust in God and His goodness.

One more glance outside of the 'office' window to hopefully catch my little pigeon-toed wanderer only to see a couple of vehicles still snow covered from last night's flurries. There were no leaves on the trees which made it much easier to see the parking lot. The white garage doors that lined the west side of the lot were all closed. I wondered if somewhere along Sebastian's adventures he had been 'caught' up in one for a night or two. That safe harbor would at least protect him from the elements and critters that roamed about.

This whole ordeal was a definite test of faith. By now, God and I had daily conversations on the subject. More often than not, my anxieties overpowered any messages He wanted to give me. It was a challenge to still my heart and mind and just listen.

Some days I would 'release' Sebastian to Him trusting that He would keep him safe; along with the angels and saints. "Please keep him safe, warm and dry." I would plead while on my knees next to my bed. And then some days, I would take back the release and carry the burden myself, letting my humanness take over once again. Was this one of the reasons I was childless? I was feeling just a tad irresponsible.

This is the pond just north of us at Barbara Key Park. Sebastian was on his way back from having walked on the ice. A few weeks later we went back and when he dipped his paw on the 'ice,' it was no longer ice, but cold water.

The Pet Psychic
An Assurance

I believe cats to be spirits come to earth.
A cat, I am sure, could walk on a cloud
without coming through.

Jules Verne

Fast forward to January, 2010. I had been referred to a "Pet Psychic" whom I promptly called as soon as I could and made a phone appointment. Fortunately, the psychic was doing a service project during the month of January and wasn't charging for her readings. There IS a God! I couldn't wait to talk to her. His angels were working their magic.

In all your ways acknowledge Him.
And He will make your paths straight.

Proverbs. 3:6

"Hello?" And I went on to describe my situation trying not to give away too much information so as to 'test her authenticity.'

"I see him walking away...there's a dark energy around him... There's also a Preserve." She went on to inform me that he was a very capable cat with a strong personality. Ah yes, that would be Fen Nature Preserve just west and north of Barbara Key Park. She was right on track. Maybe the "dark energy" was all of those things I had lost or let go of over the past two years. And then I wondered if it was the status of my father's health and his impending passing. The doctor had given him eight months and when Sebastian left we were in our fifth month. There were certainly a lot of possibilities to fulfill that observation.

"He's got a lot of moxie." She went on to identify him and his demeanor.

"Well, yes, I could see that in him. A rather proud cat." She said. I agreed, she didn't want to hurt my feelings, "but he's moved on."

Oh no! I didn't want to hear that. I shuddered inside at the sound of the words. She added that he hadn't attached himself to anyone. So, there was hope!

"I see layers of sadness in your apartment unit about knee high and if you had a party, it would raise the energy level. He would be attracted to this." Hmmmm…layers of sadness. Considering all of the events that had transpired, I could understand that.

There was the job loss, the divorce, learning of Dad's terminal cancer, Sebastian's disappearance, the freak accident with my car deeming it a 'total loss,' being blessed in having the funds available to purchase a 'new' car. With no job; no loan. Traveling back-and-forth to Platteville helping Dad when I could. There were just a few stress points in the mix. Calling on God's strength and knowing that He is in control got me through it all. He never gives us more than we can handle.

Is that all it would/might take to do the trick? And where was that energy going to come from?

In an update, shortly before this reading, my father had passed on the 20th of December and the services were held on the 26th. I had taken on a seasonal part-time job in retail but found I couldn't finish my term of employment. The holidays can be so hectic to begin with and then with the loss of my father, it really put a cloak of sadness and upset around an otherwise joyful and exciting time of the year. Sending out Christmas cards was little more than a fleeting thought. So, why or how could I get up my energy level to even consider having a party? I was grappling with the 'joy' in life…or of the season for that matter. We all went through the motions. Christmas came and went.

The pet psychic even went so far as to describe the house in detail of where he had been taken in. She also noted that he was "sparing me of something…" In reflection, I decided that he was sparing me from

Still Lost! *Orange Tabby cat, has a blue collar and purple, heart-shaped tag, "Sebastian." If you **SEE** this animal, please call me at 123-456-7890. Last seen Nov. 7.*

the stress of having to take him back and forth to my hometown to visit Dad. I've already discussed how upsetting that would have been for Sebastian and that much more upsetting for me during that time.

Up until the time of Dad's passing, he had gone from the hospital to the nursing home, back home, then to the hospital and then we learned that he had formalized an order to "not resuscitate." It was back to the nursing home. We knew the end was near. His last days were pretty much spent in a comatose state. It was time to let go and let God take him home. It would have been selfish of us to want him to stay here with us and at 86 years old, he had led a full life. He was more than ready to go and meet his Maker. We had to release him as he would be spending the holidays with Mother, and his Mother, brothers and so many other relatives and townspeople he had paid his last respects to at the funeral home over the years. Now it was his time for his sendoff and reception. His mission here on earth was finished. He would meet his reward.

Back to the phone reading…"He's content." The psychic stated describing Sebastian's mental and physical state.

No, no. How could he possibly be content with anyone else? Had they taken him to McDonald's for ice cream after an unleashed romp in the park? Did they even take him to the park? C'mon… Did they get up with him in the night and stay with him while he did his thing and then play with him before going back to bed? Wasn't I always available when he wanted to crawl up on my lap for a stroke or two and a hug? Wasn't his food dish always filled? I felt betrayed. Twist that knife into my heart, will you.

Enter Sidney!
Second Healer and Companion

When they are among us, cats are angels.
George Sand

The January blues slid into February and I was feeling pretty lowly. Having realized what a comfort Sebastian had been with his unconditional love, I scavenged Craig's List for kittens to be given away. I needed a strong dose of fluffy unconditional love and affection.

On a Tuesday, I found an ad with four black kittens. Thee cutest little things you'd ever seen. I immediately fell in love with one of the four and decided I would call him or her "Sidney" after Sidney Poitier. It was a unisex type name anyway. I called the number on the ad several times and left messages and finally reached the party that next evening.

"The last two were picked up this afternoon about 1:00 PM." said the advertiser.

"Oh no, you're kidding! You didn't get my messages?" I pleaded.

"No, I'm sorry ma'am." He sounded disappointed as he tried to sympathize but his advertisement paid off so he was happy in the end.

"Oh. That's okay." I was so disappointed. My hopes were shot. I still liked the name Sidney, though. The emptiness in my heart remained.

A few more days of searching the 'List' and I came across another ad and called.

"I have ten cats and need to start getting rid of them." The lady told me over the phone in a sweet, soft voice. She had to have a sweet, soft voice; she was a cat lover!

"How about if I come out to see them Wednesday evening?" That worked.

Wednesday evening and I was excited and looking forward to checking out her menagerie. The little white house was tucked away in the woods of a suburb about a half hour away. I knocked on the door and this short little lady with the dark shoulder length hair answered. I saw a few black large fluffs scramble into the other room and then some went racing down the stairs to the basement. Joyce was very friendly and easy to talk to. She led me into her living room where we sat and visited. She figured she would have to move in a year or two and had to start letting go of her brood or clowder. Joyce sat on the loveseat and I on the couch.

It wasn't long and one of her feline friends came into the room and put her front paws on the corner glass topped coffee table. She poised her head to get a better look at this stranger and I was smitten. Here was this beautifully marked black-and-white kitty checking me out. My first impression, "The Eyes have it." There's my Sidney, I thought. She jumped up on the arm of the loveseat next to Joyce and crouched down to get a better view. After a few moments she gave me one of those slow blinks of the eyes.

"Did you see that?" Joyce inquired.

"Yes, I did." I answered with a big smile on my face.

Joyce and I were familiar with a cat's mannerisms and when they do a slow blink, in cat language, that means they adore or like what they see and trust you. Otherwise known as a 'kitty kiss.' She definitely liked what she saw and I certainly liked what I saw, too! Before I left 'Daisy,' the name Joyce gave her, she had come close enough to sniff the leg of my slacks and then collapse at my feet inviting me to rub her belly. It was quite evident that she accepted me into her 'space.' For such a skittish kitten, I was quite impressed. Joyce was impressed, too. I made arrangements to come back on Friday to pick her up so I could spend quality time with her over the weekend. I had been working at a temporary position and didn't have the time available to me that I had earlier.

FEBRUARY 5th: Pick up 'Daisy' aka 'Sidney.' Joyce had warned me that she was a 'talker.' She had even checked with the vet to see if her gibberish was normal and the vet assured her Daisy was fine. Nothing to worry about. With me living alone, it would be nice to have a 'talker.' Daisy was also a cuddler at night! Wonderful! I hit the jackpot! And what a sweetheart. I know it was just two days, but Friday night finally arrived and I was really looking forward to my (our) newest addition.

I was reminded of another reading I had had done almost a year earlier and was asked, "Why are you thinking of another cat?" My immediate reaction was, "What? No! One's enough." I was forewarned that there would be another cat in my future...

Friday evening came and I was ready to welcome this new little resident into my heart and home.

In Joyce's kitchen, the cat carrier was resting on a chair as Joyce and I visited further and it wasn't long and Daisy/Sidney had climbed right in...! Sure, cats are curious, but was she also trying to tell me something? I marvel at their sensitivities.

If we could just pay a little more attention to our animals, they can sense and see things that we can't and for our protection. Joyce informed me that one night there was a man outside the living room window; a peeper of sorts and a few of the cats became very restless and came to her aid. The man disappeared and hopefully will never return. Cats have very keen eyesight and can hear sounds not audible to us and have also been known to alert their owners of other life threatening incidents; gas leaks, fire, smoke, etc.

They are also much more aware of spiritual entities that are in our midst. Case in point; Sebastian would sit on the arm of the loveseat with his back to me and look around the kitchen or ceiling following something of interest... I couldn't see anything. Also there is a chemical that is released between owner and animal. It's called oxytocin. It's a chemical that raises the endorphin level, lower one's blood pressure and can actually extend the life of a person. Need I say more? Joyce and I had bonded and I assured her I would keep her posted of Daisy's adjustment to her new residence. She gave me her papers and we were off.

The drive on the way home went very well. Joyce had warned me that when Daisy was driven down to Chicago to be spayed that she and the other accompanying cat cried and carried on so. She felt so badly for them but knew it had to be done.

On this ride, however, Daisy fared very well. I also had doubled up an afghan completely covering the carrier so as to keep out the light (it was night anyway) but also to keep out the cold. We were experiencing a few of those sub-zero days then.

Home! As soon as I opened the carrier, Daisy scampered under the couch...and stayed there throughout the night. And didn't emerge Saturday morning. Nor Saturday afternoon. It wasn't until Saturday evening that she finally, slowly, emerged and found the feeding dish and water. She immediately took to the litter box and I imagined she was a little surprised to find she was the only thing missing from this new habitat. There were toys all over the place. A stuffed catnip mouse here; a ball of yarn there; a small ball with a bell in it that tinkled when it rolled was in front of a towel-lined basket just her size. She might have thought, "Man, this is a pretty neat place. There is even a long tube in the other room that crackles when I crawl into it. Hey! I LIKE this place; I could really feel comfortable here and call this 'home.' And my new owner likes to cuddle and pet me. At bedtime, when I jump up on her bed and before I drop off to sleep I rest my head on her arm and stare into her eyes until I can't keep my little peepers open any longer. Then I outstretch one paw touching her arm, face, or neck."

After a few nights, I decide to 'baptize' Daisy and change her name to 'Sidney.' When I call her, I'll sometimes call out "Sidney Loooooou."

This is my Sidney. She was born May 26, 2010, and loves to crawl into small places and nap. She's as sweet as she looks. Her white fur is oh so soft and white.

The Search Continues...
Another Phone Call

*How we behave toward cats here below deter-
mines our status in heaven.*

Robert A. Heinlein

DAY 143: It was Holy Week! Tuesday afternoon and I was sitting
in a realtor's office taking one step further into establishing a more
permanent home for myself and Sidney. My present residence was for
sale and I didn't know when that was going to happen so I thought I
should be prepared and see what was out there and available.

In the meantime, I was also praying that Sebastian would find his
way back before my present unit sold and I would have to move. Peg,
the realtor, and I had this most delightful exchange of animal stories;
she with her dogs and me with my cats. We also shared how we had
met up with different mediums and psychics. I was telling her all over
again of how this one assured me I would "have Sebastian for a long
time." I held onto that prediction that Sebastian would come home
someday.

The weather was warming up nicely and the realtor had even stated that if Sebastian 'escaped' from me, that he would 'escape' again.

I just felt in my heart of hearts that this would be the week. How
would I find him? Would he be healthy looking? Would he be scarred
in some way? Would his paws be all torn up? Would he recognize me?
I read and heard that cats have similar senses that dogs do and can find
their way home by scent. It would be just a matter of time...and luck. I
had also heard of a dog that returned after five years and the owner had
moved FOUR times in the meantime. Phenomenal! Since we lived in
the suburbs of Chicago, would he turn out to be my 'Miracle Cat?' It

wasn't as if he hadn't had a lot of cleared land to navigate. There were also subdivisions and traffic and so much movement all the time. A country cat lost in the city...

"Less than 5% of lost cats return home," read the Arm & Hammer cat litter box. My frustration arose once again as I quietly pledged never to let Sebastian out again. I just knew in my heart that he would return. I wouldn't accept any other option. I just wouldn't.

DAY 144: Wednesday of that week and my hair appointment was scheduled for 4:30 PM. My beautician and I were having a nice exchange, as usual, and I told her all about Sidney and hopes of Sebastian returning. While she clipped away my cell rang but I was unable to pick it up. I did have their number now in my phone and would call 'them' back as soon as I could.

"I hope he comes back." Those were my beautician's parting comments. I checked my phone for the call that I missed and called the number right away.

"Are you still missing your cat?" The fellow asked. Here we go again...

"Yes!" I replied anxiously and held my breath in anticipation.

"I think we have him here." Ah...Music to my ears. Oh please, Lord, I hope it's him.

"Oh!! Give me your address and I'll be there as soon as I can!"

The location was about five miles north of where I lived. I couldn't believe it, but then I'd been on a wild goose chase a time or two before...

Would he look like my 'ole Sebastian; the way I remembered him?
Or worse, would he remember me?

Sebastian's Back!
My Miracle Cat!

One small cat changes coming home to an
empty house to coming home.

Pam Brown

Holy Week! I reflected on its significance: the week when the long awaited Messiah was being hailed as the King of Kings and Lord of Lords. The Great Healer.

Pulling into the drive, I saw several two story units built next to one another in units of two. The afternoon sun was bright and the branches on the trees were just beginning to sprout of buds. There in a driveway to my right was a young man sitting in a folding chair strumming his guitar. Lost in his interpretation and with his headphones on, he really wasn't aware of me or the car. I stopped the car, rolled down the window and called out,

"Can you tell me where 410 is?" I asked. He had removed his headphones and was able to help me out.

"Go around the corner here…" He pointed a finger off to his right.

"Thank you." I said and slowly drove through the buildings once again.

There it was; 410. I slid the envelope of photos out from under some other paperwork on the passenger side and pulled out a few so as to verify that I was the owner and that, indeed, this would be Sebastian.

I slowly walked up the sidewalk to the screen door. As I peered through the door, I could see a beautiful black-and-white cat sitting on the back of the couch just a couple of feet from the front door. Then, beyond the screen door, I saw a young woman on another couch sitting with her husband. As soon as she saw me she got up and approached the door with him following close behind.

There was a large front window that appeared to go from floor to ceiling where a couple of other cats were walking about. This young lady and her roommate apparently were cat lovers also and would understand my anxiety and joy if, in fact, they did have Sebastian.

"We've got him in the garage." She went in and brought out a black cat carrier. Through the black mesh I caught sight of this enraged animal. She grabbed him and pulled him out holding him away from her as he was quite upset. It was Sebastian's coloring, but with all the fluff, growling, hissing and snarling, I wasn't too sure…

We visited a bit and I discovered that they already had four cats and this cat had been milling around outside their unit all afternoon. She said she had checked the computer for the ongoing ad I had placed in the local paper and gave me a call.

Now it just so happened that the week before, I had received a copy of my *Cat Fancy Magazine* and as I was paging through trying to find a look-a-like of Sidney to show Holly, the waitress at the local pizza restaurant, I caught a quick glance of a photo on the back page and did a double-take. There was my Sebastian! I had sent in a photo or two and apparently the editors felt that it was as cute as I thought and published it. A complete and delightful surprise! So now my Sebastian was also a celebrity. Holly and I had 'bonded' of sorts as she had a couple of cats that she wanted to find homes for. I had told her of the void I felt now that my Sebastian had been on 'hiatus.'

Turns out, when I was leaving for Platteville back in December, I told Erika, across the hall of our building, about my Father's passing and how long I would be gone. I told her then about the ad that had expired. Her husband worked with one of the local newspapers so she excitedly offered to have Chris drop my ad off to the Classified Department and they would run it indefinitely. Hallelujah! Thank you, Lord!

Back to this thrilling find…

Again, I wasn't sure about this wild animal. For some naive reason, I thought I would find a docile, friendly cat. He was friendly, all right. The young lady assured me of that. However, this 'beast' was not something or someone I expected.

I put my hand near the animal so he could recognize my scent. That seemed to settle him some. When she pulled the cat out of the carrier the sun hit the fur that was standing on end, lose and flying all over. As she handled him, I was looking for any signs of familiarity. I remembered the bite he had received the summer before and checked out the back side of his right paw. The bite had irritated him so; he had licked a 2" by 1" strip clear to the skin. The new fur would be a different shade.

"That's HIM!" I happily exclaimed.

Sebastian was back!

The Resurrection? The Renewal? The Rebirth? Hallelujah!! Thank you, Lord!

> *Indeed the very hairs of your head are all numbered. Do not fear; you are of more value than many sparrows*
>
> **Luke 12:7**

He answered my prayers and reaffirmed my faith big time.

Hallelujah! He's back! I wanted to shout it to the world.

Kathy, the young, blonde woman who held Sebastian, suggested we put him back into the carrier and unload him into my car. That worked quite nicely. I took down her name and asked if they had a favorite restaurant. She quickly turned my reward down and being a cat owner, she was just as pleased that Sebastian was back where he belonged. I was so grateful for their help and phone call.

As soon as Sebastian picked up my scent in the car, he immediately settled down and knew he was 'home.' I couldn't believe it. Sebastian was back.

"I love you, a bushel and a peck, a bushel and a peck and a hug around the neck." I sang as we slowly made our way home. All the while I gently petted him as he crouched on the console in between the seats. I believe he was happy to be back 'home', too.

I wondered what he had been through. Where he'd been and with whom? Were they nice to him? His collar was different than I remembered and it was well worn. Had they tied him up and had he tried to run? I grimaced as I thought what caused the fur to be gone all along his neckline. It appeared to be a hard fought 'necklace' of survival. Had they broken his spirit as they do with horses? I wanted to hug and hold him all night.

Once Sidney was safely settled behind the spare bedroom door, Sebastian was free to reacquaint himself with his surroundings. It took him awhile to warm back up to me. Since they have such an acute sense of smell, I'm sure he picked up on another cat in our midst. At one point in the evening he was resting on my bed and I went in to have a little talk with him about his new roommate. I got on my knees alongside the bed and began…"Sebastian, I have to tell you something. There's another kit-…" There was a growling.

"Meoooooww! HISsssssssssssssss! Growl!" I got just a little closer and he went into defense mode!

"Meoooooww! HISsssssss! Growwl" He then jumped up and cuffed me twice on the cheek with his paw letting out a few more disdainful and alarming meooowws. Then he bounded off the back side of the bed. Apparently he wasn't ready for any friendly chat yet.

"O-kaayyyy, I guess we're not ready to talk." And I exited the room.

He needed more time to collect himself. Yes, he definitely knew there was another resident and wasn't at all happy with me having replaced him. Well? I was lonely and besides, this way he would have a companion and playmate. I don't think he saw it this way right now. Lord knows what my poor Sebastian had been through and now he felt incensed and betrayed. And I was willing to give him that time. As much time as he needed to feel comfortable. My Sebastian was back HOME.

I got on my e-mail as soon as I could and sent out a short message to my friends that "Sebastian's back!" Only I couldn't wait for their responses. I either called a few yet that night or began calling the next

This angel has a cat in her loving, protective arms. One of my sister-in-laws gave it to me for Christmas 2009, when Sebastian was missing.

day. I was SO excited! My baby was back. And I wanted the whole world to know about it!

Some of my e-mail responses were:

"I'm so glad no one ate him, too. That's such a gross thought but I have heard that it does happen. Anyway, enjoy being with your cat "kids.""—Linda H.

"This is a miracle story. Animals have a gift to wander for months and get back to the people who love them. If he could talk I am sure he would have so many stories to tell you. God is good and He does miracles every day. How long has Sebastian been gone? Give him lots of kisses from me. I am so happy you have your family together again. He and Sidney will have years together. Love to you, Laurie"

"Amen! So happy you have your cat back. I hope he isn't too much the worse for wear. I bet someone took him in and he 'escaped' from there. Keep a good eye on him." —Barbara N.

"Hi Kay, I am so happy for you. When I read your email the following Bible verse came to my mind. Psalm 27:13. I am confident of this: "I will see the goodness of the Lord in the land of the living." What a nice person to return your kitty. Sweet dreams, Love, Anita"

"Amazing!"—my sister

"Kay - Thank God! I am so happy to hear this. I hope you're not going to let him out again. Also, you could have a microchip put in him and the other cat in case they get out sometime. That way they could be identified if they end up in a shelter. I'm sure you must be so relieved to have your little kitty back again. Hope the kitties will get along. You're doing the right thing to keep them separated at first. When I first introduced our new cats I had kept one in the carrier so they could look at each other but with protection in case someone went crazy. Anyway, this is the best news I've heard today. Thanks for the update!"—Linda H.

"How terrific! Reminds me of the movies the boys love when the animals returned home."—Donna L.

"I am so glad. I hope they both get along now. Don't let him out any more. Hope all is well with you. Love and hugs,"—Janet xoxox

"Sebastian" by Kay Clark
This shot was the photo selected and published in the May, 2010 issue of "Cat Fancy" magazine.

Adjustments

Sebastian Tries to Settle in...
Hey! I'm not Alone!

A cat is a lion in a jungle of small bushes.
Folk saying from India

That first night, he was pretty restless. Pacing the floor, going from the bedroom to the living room and back. Then he'd check me out. Sebastian wasn't ready to forgive and wasn't ready to join me in bed yet. And that was okay, too. Not until the next night and then it was at the bottom of the bed. Maybe, he, too, missed me and was trying to accept the fact that he had to share the limelight.

The following night, though, he came up to me and gave me a head butt and then with both hands, I gently massaged his neck and began petting him, nuzzling his forehead with mine telling him how happy I was that he was home and safe now. I still couldn't believe he was home and yet I knew he would be back. My furry buddy was back.

When he would come back, here I thought I would boo-hoo my eyes out in sheer joy. But I was able to contain myself and still thank the Lord and His angels for bringing him back home to me. Sebastian had enough to deal with let alone a hysterical 'mother.'

The following day, besides making phone calls, I couldn't wait to tell Holly, the waitress at the local Pizza Hut. She was so expressive and I knew she would be just about as excited as I was. Holly knew and observed that every time I came in, I would be writing in my notebook. She had encouraged me to indeed, write my story and tell others about the endearing relationship between Sebastian and Me!

Holly had her back to me talking to another customer when I arrived. When she spotted me she made her way over to where I was already seated and exclaimed, "We were just talking about you and your cat." (And this was before I came into the restaurant.) I was impressed!

"Have you read my latest e-mail?" I excitedly inquired I was just beaming with excitement and could hardly contain myself.

"I got the one about the photo being published." she said as she leaned into and mechanically slid down the back of the seat opposite me. It appeared she'd had a busy day so far. She was a very good waitress.

"Oh, no. This is the one I sent just last night." I countered.

"No, I haven't." She replied as she stared blankly back at me.

"Sebastian's back!"

Her eyes grew wide as she appeared shell-shocked!

"Oh, my gosh!" she exclaimed. "Really? That's wonderful! Where has he been all this time?" she continued.

I really couldn't tell her because I really didn't know. I did know that the pads of his paws were soft and pink so I figured he had been taken in somewhere for the winter. Thank the Good Lord! As my good news sunk in, she became more animated. I, myself, wanted to shout it to the World!

"Amazing!" was all my sister could transmit on her iPod.

"It's a miracle!" Another friend responded.

"I'm soooo happy for you!" came another e-mail.

"I thought he was gone…" another friend confessed.

I couldn't wait to get to church and tell the other ladies. After church, one of the ladies inquired, "Where has he been all this time?" Again, I couldn't answer. (He hadn't left a forwarding address.) And no one had actually pulled up in front of my building, rang the buzzer and told me they had Sebastian.

"Hoo-ray!" Announced another as she raised both fists in the air. She was as pleased and excited as I was. And then there was the fellow who sold me my car… I dialed the number to the dealership.

"Is Roger there?" I couldn't wait to tell him the good news.

"I told you he would come back." He was pleased being a dog person, himself. He's also a salesman and a very positive and upbeat fellow.

This whole experience has definitely been a spiritual journey of hope and faith, the Love and Grace of our Lord--and prayer for miracles. Me, trying to release my faith to the Universe, trusting in God, St Francis, St. Anthony and enlisting the help of all the angels in heaven. And now I've been blessed with not one but two of God's loving little fluffy creatures!

Sidney:
"To know me is to love me"
The Eyes Have it!

Cats teach us to ignore our
mistakes and carry on.

Sidney is my multi-colored cat. She has such a beautiful face with sharp contrasting colors. She knows her name and is a well-behaved communicator. Her original 'mother' even asked the vet if it was normal for a cat to chatter and carry on so but the vet assured her she was fine.

When Sidney came into my life, Sebastian was still on hiatus and I welcomed her banter. She was also a cuddler at night and would lie on my outstretched arm facing me on her left side and me lying on my right side with her head resting on my arm. We would gaze into one another's eyes and drift off but not before her outstretched paw touched my chin or face. It was as if she needed that reassurance. And I loved it. Still do.

Sidney is full and fluffy and twice the size of Sebastian and half as old. I've never known of a cat to lick her lips as often as she does. As soon as the refrigerator door opens, there's Sidney with her unofficial snooper's license. She's my beautiful, melt-your-heart sweetheart. It has taken over a year but she will finally jump up next to me on the couch and curl up sometimes rolling over and inviting me to rub her belly. Did I say invite? I meant beg. She will follow me around in anticipation of me stopping just long enough to give her a quick rub. It almost appears she can't get enough of the belly rub and will swish back and forth against my leg before doing her 'drop and roll' slowly writhing about with all fours in the air rocking back and forth. When she stretches out, I swear she is near three feet long. That's a sign of trust.

Patience is a virtue and Sidney is certainly patient when it comes to meal time and allowing Sebastian first dibs on the food dish. She knows better as Sebastian has often declared himself the 'alpha cat' or dominant one. Sidney will quietly hang back hunched down and wait until Sebastian has had his fill. Then she cautiously approaches the dish and takes her turn. I think she realizes that Sebastian and I have a special relationship; one that was forged long before she came on board and will watch as he and I will cuddle on the couch. I don't get the sense that Sidney is jealous but she will from time to time attack Sebastian. I think it's mostly a playful gesture as Sebastian will be the one to return the attack and bite her neck. Then squeals of anguish will ring out and the fur will literally fly with Sebastian ending up with a mouthful of fur. Yuk! Spitter, sputter.

It's Sidney who will instigate a race around and over the couches and from room to room. They need their exercise and are really good for one another. And then you'll see Sidney giving Sebastian a tongue bath as Sebastian tries to sleep away the hours. I believe Sebastian really enjoys this but Sidney can get carried away and Sebastian has to become firm and will sometimes just walk away. Enough already, Sidney.

It's comforting and a Kodak moment when you catch them both sleeping, one practically on top of the other. Then you know they really, really do tolerate and like one another and enjoy the company they keep.

Sidney has a wonderful personality and has taught me a lot about what it means to love someone. In my observations, I've seen her submit to Sebastian and his dominance—and with patience. I don't know that she keeps score or is vengeful. I don't see that in her. How does one define unconditional love = Sidney. Sidney is unconditional love incarnate. All she asks is that I scratch her ears on both sides and when she rolls over give her a good massage on her tummy and she's happy.

We have a ritual; when I get out of the shower, she's right there almost between my legs and catching a few drips before she leaps up on to the commode and begs me to give her a good scratch behind her ears and working a massage down her furry and fluffy body. She won't let up with the begging until I do. After a few sessions of maneuvering along her long, round frame, she is satisfied and goes into the other room. Of course, after each long stroke I have to wipe my hands of cat hair and deposit them in the wastebasket nearby. I'm glad we have this ritual. I don't feel so guilty when I pay so much attention to Sebastian. This is a special thing just between Sidney and I and she loves it.

Sidney knows her name. If I don't see her around, I call out her name and in three tries, here she will come, loping along meowing in answer to my call to her. A few taps on the couch and she will jump up and acclimate herself among the covering and nestle down next to me. Or she will jump up on the bed and if I signal to her by tapping on my bare arm a few times, she will come right up, plop down and lay her head on my arm while I pet her and lightly scratch her neck and head. I try to be mindful of Sebastian's location so as not to insight a confrontation. Sebastian can get jealous. Again, the 'alpha cat' coming to the surface. At about this time Sebastian would no doubt still be curled up on the couch sleeping away. Eventually, they will switch places or Sidney will end up on the foot of the bed or hunkered down in the bend of my legs. They are so comforting. They don't belch, burp or fart and I don't have to worry at all about the toilet lid being left up.

I love the fact that they are as independent as they are so I can come and go. All I have to do is make sure there is plenty of food and water, the TV or radio on and a light and they are good to go. I like to know that they are comforted and not completely abandoned. And they are good company for one another.

Sidney has taught me not to hold grudges. Let things go. Don't hang on to them. They are old news. Nothing can be done about them and it does more harm to hold onto them anyway. I can't help but think this may forge a stronger bond between Sebastian and Sidney. Sidney is the bigger cat for forgiving and letting go of little irritations. Although I believe this just may be in their natural demeanor. Sidney has taught me humility and that being an 'observer' isn't so bad. Her never-ending 'snooper's license' and natural curiosity has taught me that I should never get bored with life. Always be curious and look for the fun and contentment that is there to be found.

In the dining room there are three colorful cubes with holes carved out on three sides of each cube. These are such that when linked together make a great tunnel and walkway to frolic in. Sidney loves to curl up in any one of them and take a little cat nap. This is where I can sometimes find her if she comes up missing. Sebastian will sometimes observe her comfort and tranquility, disturb and aggravate her to the point where she will get up and leave her nice warm enclosure. Then Sebastian will take up residence and take his nap. Sidney just walks away and finds another spot to hunker down and catch a few zzzzzz's. I marvel at her 'fight or flight' attitude and how she so easily chooses 'flight.' I think we could all learn something from their behaviors. Wouldn't it be much easier, in some cases, (road rage?) to just let things go? I think we'd all be better off and healthier. There would be less stomach upset; no need for acid indigestion medicines. No ulcers, gurd, etc. And that's just the tip of the iceberg. No eating disorders... the list goes on and on.

Sometimes throughout the day, I will let Sebastian out to play in the hallway on our floor. I keep the door ajar so he can bop back in anytime he feels the need. He'll make a beeline for the door when he hears someone enter the building or leaves their apartment. Most any disturbance will do the trick. He's friendly but not that friendly and for this I'm grateful. He will either head butt the door or just pounce on it and will come back home. He most always keeps the doorknob of our unit in sight.

While out in the hall he'll writhe and roll on the carpet out there. It's more of an indoor/outdoor material and more abrasive than the carpet in our unit. Sidney is happier to stay inside and will crouch about six feet from the door and be the watchmen waiting for Sebastian's return. It's as if she can't play or relax without him around.

Then I'll check the door, opening it and sometimes Sebastian will be ready to return but not before a long stretch. Then he'll be warmly greeted by Sidney who will give him kitty kisses and nudge his face with her nose. Then she's fine and will return to normal. Until then, she's on 'Sebastian Watch'.

How can you not love this face?

God made kittens and cats for a purpose. Some will refute that. I had heard of a legend about the cat. In the manger, when the baby Jesus was wrapped in swaddling clothes among the straws of hay, it was the cat that curled up next to Him and comforted him with its purr to help him sleep. The Blessed Mother touched his head as in a blessing and that's where the 'M' pattern comes from on top of their heads. What a wonderful thought.

I am well aware of the spiritual connection between my cat friends and things of a spiritual and celestial nature. Often I will notice the cats following something around them with their eyes as if it were flying or landing and then will go on about their business. They can see spirits or angels and I'm sure they have seen a few in my apartment.

"Who do you see?" I'll ask with a smile and know that I am not alone and comforted by my protectors from the heavens as well as my two four-legged, furry sweethearts.

In Your Face
Look at Me!

You're no one until you've been
ignored by a cat.

Sidney likes to be in your face! She will walk across my keyboard a number of times while I'm working. Each time I coax her along so she doesn't disrupt my work but she still manages to hit a few keys. So while I try to collect myself, she continues on her merry way snooping around either my desk or table to see what's new; what's been untouched by her nose and needs inspecting. Then she will curl up making herself comfortable—right on my paperwork at hand. But she's so darned cute. How can I yell at her? I can't.

Then I try to play with her tail. She gets a little agitated with that and after a while will even nip me. By nipping, I mean, come at my hand with her mouth open and teeth exposed. She won't bite hard; just a nip. A love bite of sorts. It will be just enough to remind me that that isn't a thing for me to 'play' with.

Sidney's favorite spot for me to play with her is a good massage behind and around her ears or her tummy. I observed that right off from her original 'Mom' at our first meeting. Her 'Mom' was already a cat-lover but she seemed to tune in on Sidney's passions and a few brisk strokes around the ears and she was a happy and satisfied feline.

She also knows that when I'm in the restroom she has a 'captive' audience and after announcing herself and swishing her tail along my legs, she will go over to the tub next to me, plop down with her back side against the tub and collapse rolling over so as to expose her hungry tummy. Hungry as in, 'I need a good rubbing, Mom and I'm not going to leave until I've been satisfied'. Most of the time I will oblige. And then there is the shower ritual.

When Sidney hears the shower running, she knows I'm getting ready to go somewhere. She will politely crouch in waiting just outside the bathroom door as if to stand guard. When I step out of the shower, she is prompted to begin heralding her pleas which means 'I'd better get in a good scratch now before she leaves.' As I start to towel off she will jump up on the commode and continues to plea for her 'moment with mom,' anxiously anticipating my full attention and the serious massage around the ears starting there and then continue massaging on down through her fur on either side of her backbone, gently clawing my way on either side of her thick tummy. By this time she has slid down off the commode and is looking forward to and pleading for another round. I try to abide by her wishes but I have to dry off, too, and get dressed for the day.

Sidney is the second love of my life next to Sebastian, of course. Love incarnate. Heaven-sent, Band-Aids. Together they are very special companions to me. Unconditional love. And I try to divide my love and attention to both of them. But how do you 'divide' love. I think when you look into the eyes of these two, the love you feel for them is multiplied. Now you may think me daft over my little kitty friends, but I've never had children and have this heart full of love and these lucky little furry fluffs are the happy recipients of all I have to give right now. I can forgive them when they get in my face.

I understand they are a 'team.' One female and one male, which makes for great company for the two of them so when Mr. Right comes into my life, neither one of them will feel left out nor ignored. Well, maybe they'll be ignored for a bit, but not left out.

At one point, I felt that when I left the apartment and left them to their own devices, that they would feel free to really pick on one another and have a bout of some serious fist-o-cuffs. 'Not so,' I was informed. They get along quite well. Often they will curl up really close together on the couch next to me and Sidney will usually be the one to initiate a gentle tongue bath on Sebastian and do a pretty thorough job

Sebastian is certainly not above taking advantage of getting in my face either!

of it, too. When he's had enough, he will perk up and signal to Sidney to 'back off.'

Sometimes Sebastian will be the initiator. And then as though it will remind him of the spell he has cast over her, he will go for her neck and really give a few good bites. Within moments, Sidney is in 'fight mode,' lets out a few squeals and together they will tussle a little before Sebastian gets the message. Then they will separate and go to their respective 'corners' wherever that would be. As long as they are several feet away from one another all is well. It isn't long and they will once again be curled up next to one another.

They remind and continue to teach me to let go of people who might have offended me and forgive them. Basically, they are good and decent people and may just have had a bad day. I just happen to be in the cross fires. And even if it was my fault, I should still let it go. Life is too short to harbor and hold grudges. It shortens my life and isn't good for my health. And, in five years, who's going to remember? How important was the incident anyway? That's another blessing that comes along with these two fluffy packages. They don't yell and scream if the dishes aren't done. They will, however, let me know when their food dish is empty. And that's ok, too. Then both of them will be in my face! Big time.

Sidney's First Venture Outside
A Hypothetical Situation

I had read where it's important to try to socialize your shy, skittish pets and since Sidney had been housebound and terribly skittish, even around her previous mother, I thought I would take her outside and let her play in the front or back yard along with Sebastian. Now Sebastian was quite comfortable doing this and seeing the two of them together outside would surely be a sight to see.

Previously when Sidney would get out to even just the hallway of the building, she would become disoriented as soon as she was out of sight and would begin meowing loudly, which could have been disturbing to the other tenants. I didn't need that! So this time, I stayed close to her as we descended the stairs and I opened the door to the lobby.

"C'mon Sidney." I invited her to come through the doorway. She just looked up at me and then the opened door. 'What should I do now, Mom?' seemed to be her thoughts. Since it appeared she would still be safe, she hesitated and then slowly walked through the door. Sebastian needed no invitation. He was already there and awaiting the opening of the door to the outside.

The first door closed and the three of us were now in the lobby. Sidney was a little shell-shocked and started to meow her concern as to what was going to happen next. This was a whole new view for her. She looked at the windows and knew she wasn't too far from the big, bad, world. Sebastian couldn't wait to launch outside.

I opened the door to the outside revealing the long sidewalk to the parking lot and the row of cars. There were bushes on either side of the walk and then just grass. Again I had to convince her to come outside. Sebastian had no problem in this area and began to chew on the blades of grass looking up every so often keeping an eye on Sidney.

"C'mon Sidney." I again invited her outside. She wouldn't move and was just overwhelmed with this idea of freedom. You'd think she was on the brink of a cliff and ready to take quite a tumble into space in a free fall not knowing where she was going to land. Ever so slowly, she crept outside and crouched down on the slab of cement seemingly petrified. Sidney looked all around as if someone were going to snatch her or worse yet, attack her. She was in defense mode.

"It's okay, Sidney, You can come out and play." Sebastian came up to her and was nose-to-nose with her letting her know that 'the water was fine.' Then he walked away and around the bushes following the line of brush around the front of the building. I wasn't too worried about him. Ever since he had run away, somehow his adventure left quite an imprint on him and he didn't want to wander too far from home. He knew life with Mom was much better than exploring in unfamiliar places. He knew and appreciated the warmth and comfort that awaited him when he got back to the apartment and wasn't about to forego that luxury. Sebastian also realized that along with a nice bed came food and water so there was no need to hunt and risk injury. And besides, he loves his mom and she loves him.

Sidney started walking out beyond the bush in search of Sebastian. She didn't want him to get out of her sight. Sebastian turned and spotted her and came galloping over towards her so as to demonstrate what she could do without fear of harm. Sidney was still somewhat nervous as Sebastian playfully bumped into her almost toppling her over.

I started out trekking through the grass trying to make Sidney feel a little more comfortable with the feel of the grass under her paws but she wouldn't have any of it and quickly sprinted toward the sidewalk seeking relief. However, this surface, too, was unfamiliar to her and she stopped short before making a beeline to the opened door. I thought I would prop it open just in case she wanted to seek refuge.

She wasn't ready to play and instead, announced her dissatisfaction with a loud meow. It echoed in the hallway so I took out my keys, unlocked the second door and guided her through it. She gratefully went through it and scampered up the stairs. Once at the top of the stairs, again she let out a meow as if to exclaim, 'what do I do now, Mom?' I ascended the stairs and started down the hall towards our door, unlocked the door with Sidney at my feet and we both went into the apartment. I could almost hear her 'whewsh' and imagined her wiping her brow as if barely escaping a serious challenge and near calamity.

In the long run, I guess the way this whole scenario played out was a good thing. Any curiosity that she might have had about the outdoors was satisfied. Now I just hoped she didn't accept this as a tease and insist on going out again. I know, it would be my fault, right? Although she did appear extremely reticent about going too far so maybe that would all right, too.

Now that I think on it, maybe that wasn't such a good idea. I mean, what if Sidney decided to take off. I remember reading that they have a difficult time focusing on things right in front of their eyes. Things at a distance, they wouldn't have so much of a problem with. And they are not ones to turn and look both ways when crossing streets. Oh Lord, I don't know what I would do if one of them darted out in front of a car and was hit in our complex. There were numerous buildings with lots of parking lots and garages.

Before Sebastian ran away he still had quite a bit of curiosity, vim and vigor in him and had no problem crossing the street and exploring in parking lots across the way. I believe that was one of my biggest frights when he took off. How many streets had he crossed to get to where he was when I found him? There were several. I mean lots of streets where lots of cars would be traveling throughout the day. Some would be traveling way too fast to stop for a cat sprinting across in front of them. And then what if a car did stop and caused a chain reaction among the cars behind it? I immediately put that thought out of my mind. Sebastian was home now. Safe. So forget it. Let go of such horrific thoughts. God and His angels protected him and got him back to you unscathed, unscarred, unharmed—accept for that fur-less necklace that I believe will be permanent. What a souvenir of his Rite of Passage.

I certainly didn't entertain any, I mean ANY thoughts along those lines with Sidney. Sidney was my sweetheart. So willing to step aside and allow Sebastian his due as the 'alpha' cat. Talk about unconditional love. After a little scrap that Sebastian initiated, Sidney would retreat and go to her 'corner' curling up and taking a nap. Within a short time, she would awaken and approach Sebastian again giving him a tongue bath on the top of his head.

Sebastian Meets Sidney
Day of Reckoning

A cat's eyes are windows, enabling
us to see into another world.

Irish Proverb

Cats are territorial and if another feline enters their territory or space the standoff and what ensues can be entertaining but risky. They have already done their homework and marked the area by rubbing up against furniture, the corners of rooms and, of course, their toys in an effort to announce that 'this area is mine.' Sebastian had done this already before he left and now Sidney was in his midst. I believe that may have had something to do with why Sidney didn't come out from under the couch for so long after she arrived. However, she was used to living with several other felines so 'territory' wasn't really an issue with her. She was the only resident in her new home now and had established a certain comfort level here.

I was more concerned with Sebastian rediscovering the comforts of being home again. Sidney would just have to adjust. Sebastian had been traumatized enough so it was time to put Sidney behind the spare bedroom door with access to the litter box and a container of food and water while Sebastian had free reign.

Sebastian immediately sensed that he wasn't alone and developed an attitude. After a couple of hours, it was time to change places and remind Sidney that she wasn't being shunned but was still welcomed and a part of my life. She, too, knew that we had company and she wasn't the only one sharing this space.

I had knelt by my bed where Sebastian was laying and tried to explain to him as gently as I could that he was not alone. He wasn't very receptive at all and let me know about his feelings on the matter in no uncertain terms.

"Hissssssss, grrrrrowwwwllll," he responded when I started to tell him of our new roommate. He wasn't one bit happy about it. He was no longer the head honcho. He had voluntarily abdicated his position of authority and was not pleased as he wanted it back. I really didn't feel guilty at this show of disdain as I thought that eventually they would form a bond and be good company for one another. Sebastian didn't see it that way. He needed time to adjust and I was willing to give him that time. I hadn't known what abuse, if any, he had suffered at the hands of someone else and he certainly didn't need any more disrespect. I backed off.

For the next couple of days I took turns with each of them allowing one to explore and enjoy the comforts of 'home' while keeping the other behind a door but for short periods of time. I didn't want either of them to feel as though they were being punished.

It was a couple of days before they got a good look at one another. And there it was—the stand-off. Sidney immediately went into slow motion carefully measuring each and every step staring down her adversary/new roommate. Sebastian crouched down on full alert, eyes transfixed on Sidney glaring and following her every move.

"Hissssss," and then that unwelcomed guttural growl. Who was this invader?

"Okay, you two. Time to separate again until you get used to this arrangement." I announced as I cajoled Sidney behind the spare room door.

"It's ok, Sebastian. You live here, too." I tried to comfort and reassure him but what does an animal comprehend? I know they recognize the sound of their owners voice and the tone of your voice has a lot to do with how they respond. Sebastian was feeling more secure and familiar in his environment now and this was a good thing. I believe Sidney knew that he was here before and she would have to submit to him. Sebastian would be the 'alpha' cat. She would have to hang back and come in second. She was used to this.

For the next couple of weeks I tried to, and still continue to, give each of them equal time as far as attention and affection. Sidney loves to have her tummy rubbed and will collapse waiting for a few strokes and she is content. She will bother you until you do.

And then we share couch time. She'll curl up next to me and I will stroke her head and encircle her ears. She loves to have the fur around her ears massaged and under her neck. And then when she knows she has your full attention, she will roll over and get that bonus tummy rub. She has the most beautiful facial markings and those eyes seem to take all of your heart into her being. She is the more playful one and will instigate a chase with Sebastian so they get their exercise.

Sebastian, in the meantime, will walk right up to me and onto my lap. He will sometimes continue onto my shoulder and nestle there as he did when I first brought him home. He'll snuggle along my neck and take in every stroke along his back and tail. He's more friendly and affectionate than Sidney in that way.

Now to see the two of them play is a joy. Sidney will voluntarily jump up on the couch where Sebastian is curled up and napping and begin with a tongue bath on the head or ear. This does not disturb Sebastian. In fact, he will revel in the attention, love and affection that Sidney so freely gives to him. When he's had enough, he lets Sidney know and will go for her neck. Sidney will go into defense mode, maybe strike out. Sebastian will pause and then there's that stare. 'What are you going to do next?' If Sidney senses that Sebastian will want to get a little more serious, Sidney takes her cue, rights herself and jumps off the couch exiting to another location.

Sebastian has also been known to voluntarily give Sidney a bath and she enjoys this very much, also. Then they will often curl up next to one another with Sidney sometimes resting her head on Sebastian's rump or back-side. It's so cute to see how they've accepted one another. Now when I leave to run an errand or go away for the weekend, I feel so much better knowing that they have one another. I'm sure to keep either the TV or radio on for their comfort and a light on in the living room. They have several 'nesting' places around in each room so each one has his or her own space.

Appears they get along quite well.

Sebastian will want to go out into the hall just to exercise his position in the 'kingdom' (apartment) with Sidney dutifully crouching a few feet from the door in anticipation of his return. If both Sebastian and I are out of the apartment, Sidney will 'voice' her loneliness. I mean, come on, she did come from a household of nine other cats. She's used to having company and doesn't like to be alone. When Sebastian returns, all is well with her again.

Sidney has taught me patience and forgiveness. And both of them have taught me how to relax and it's okay to take a nap now and then. It refreshes the soul, body and mind. Maybe they're meditating and that's a good thing, too.

More Stories

Cats are Smart and Sensitive!

They understand more than we give them credit for. Tell your cat what's going on.

It was late Tuesday afternoon and I had errands to run. As usual I was taking a 'cat count' and only Sebastian was in sight wanting to go out in the hall—again. Standing in the bedroom and about ready to leave, I walked over to the cat condo where there is an opening for the kitties to go in and curl up on the carpeted little cave. No Sidney. I went back through the living room, checked the couch and loveseat— no Sidney. Sometimes she would crouch in front of the sliding glass door looking out onto the patio and trees. No, no Sidney there either. Maybe on the other side of the square cubes that are their play toys? Nada. Check the spare bedroom, now office. Look on top of the mattress against the wall. No, she usually didn't get up there unless I was in their working. Back to the bedroom and over by the far corner of the comforter. I lifted it and sure enough, there was Sidney all huddled with her behind sticking out.

"Meow!" Okay. I'll leave you alone but at least I found you, I thought. Cats don't care to be disturbed when they are sleeping. I turned and there was Sebastian in the doorway again. I thought I would play a fast one on him; "Sebastian, where's Sidney?" To my surprise Sebastian turned his head and looked in the living room and then back into the bedroom. He was really looking for her. He recognized her name. I helped him out and pointed to the end of the bed toward the floor. I've learned that pointing in a direction doesn't register either. Not even in the direction of the cat food bowl.

"Where's Sidney?" I asked one more time.

Sebastian went over to the bed and sniffed under the first corner. No Sidney. Then he went over to the other corner, sniffed and disturbed Sidney. Sidney acknowledged his touch with her nose and he walked away having found her.

I was so surprised and profusely acknowledged him for finding her for me. "Good boy! You did it. You found Sidney!"

It was time for me to leave and make a few stops to the grocery store and pharmacy. Sebastian knew I was going somewhere. I grabbed the two bags of garbage I'd put together, my purse and keys and looked down at Sebastian who wanted to go out in the worst way. He'd already been out in the hall numerous times already today. So I began the litany... "No, Sebastian. You can't go. Nooooo." He looked up at me with pleading eyes.

"No, no, no." My directive wasn't met with cooperation.

I opened the door with him bolting out into the hall. Walking to the top of the stairs I placed my bags and purse down. Sebastian went the other way and down the other staircase. All the way down and out of sight.

"Sebastian, come up here."

I stood in the middle of the hall and looked down one stairway. Not even an ear or eye peeked around the corner. I leaned over the other way and looked down the other stairway. Nothing. I waited. And waited.

Finally Sebastian sauntered toward the door on the back side of the building that I had to go out of with the garbage. He looked up at me and meowed. Should I let him out? It had been rainy and dreary all day. If I let him out it wouldn't be for long as it was still sprinkling. Cats don't like to get wet, especially this one.

Since I had left my apartment door ajar, I thought I'd best close it. I really wasn't going to be gone that long and if Sebastian wanted to stay outside, he would just have to wait until I returned. I had my list with me on what I needed so it wouldn't take too long.

I opened the one set of doors to the foyer and Sebastian went right on out. Then I opened the second door. Even though it was only about 5 o'clock, daylight savings time had started so it was dark. The cement stoop was wet and there were a few leaves that were saturated and pasted to the cement. I was hoping that once he discovered that it was sprinkling he would turn around and run back in. Not tonight. He darted out among the dampened leaves strewn along the ground under the maple tree. There really weren't too many more leaves to fall off of that tree. They had turned such a beautiful deep and bright red and when the sun hit them, they cast a pink glow against the white siding of the other patios on the adjacent building. I had already stood directly under it and savored the moment by taking a shot with my camera looking straight up the trunk capturing the branches and color- ful leaves. The tree was just beautiful. It really lent a nice covering for my bedroom window. Now I would have to be a little more careful when I got ready for bed. I would have to lower the blinds having lost my 'shade.'

Sebastian had experienced several droplets of rain on his fur and as he pranced over by the door of the other building, he shook his head as if trying to escape the moisture that would, in the end, smooth and shine up his coat ever so nicely. He didn't appreciate it at the moment and continued checking things out. I waited in hopes he would change his mind, but no, he was content to snoop around the premises.

Well, okay, buddy. I'll be back as soon as I can, I thought. It was a little after five o'clock and people would begin coming home driv- ing in the lot. As I got into my car and was driving off, I had hoped he would have the sense to stay away from them. I had just read how in- door cats, even though they were feral cats, should still not be let out as they are not acclimated to all of the dangers out in the wild. Coyotes, squirrels, rats, dogs, raccoons, you name it. Or even other cats could attack your cat so, please, if you think you're doing your cat any favors by letting them have their freedom once in a while, don't.

So what was I doing now??? I know. Don't do as I do, do as I say, okay? I called on his angels to look after him and continued on my trek. The sooner I left, the sooner I would be back. I had hoped that he had developed a healthy fear of the unknown after his solo adventure.

He had certainly changed and seemed to be more mature than before.

On my return, upon pulling into the parking lot and rounding the corner, I prayed he hadn't ventured too far from the building. As I pulled up, there he was waiting for me just off to the right of the stoop on the cement. I got out of the car, he recognized me and began his greeting and approaching me with relief as if to say, "I've been waiting for you, Mom." And "It's about time, Mom!"

He patiently waited while I opened the first door, put my bags down and unlocked the second door. Sebastian quickly sprinted up the stairs and was out of sight. Soon he came back to the top of the stairs waiting for me and together we walked to the door. Unlocking it, he shot through the door where he was happily greeted by Sidney. They will sometimes go nose-to-nose in a greeting and then he will continue on into the living room and over by the food dish. I try to keep it filled. It's almost as if it's a reward for returning home. I understand that's further incentive for them to return home as they know there will be a reward (food or a treat) that will soon be enjoyed and devoured upon their arrival. Not to mention a verbal greeting from the owner. I almost always greet him with a "how are things going?" or "what's going on out in the hall today?" Of course, he doesn't tell me but he knows I'm talking to him and welcoming him back home.

One evening he was out for several hours. When I came back he appeared to favor his right eye. Ah oh. This happens, I thought as I scolded myself thinking this would mean a trip to the vet. 'I'll wait until the morning to see what happens.'

When we walked into the apartment, there was Sidney with her kissy face welcome for Sebastian. That's the way they greet one another which is so endearing. She also noticed his eye. Sebastian was rather quiet and kept to himself the rest of the evening, which probably wasn't all that out of the ordinary but nevertheless, I kept checking his eye, which he squinted more than the other one. He'd probably brushed past a leafy tree branch and braised his eye. At least I hoped it was leafy. I couldn't see any scratch or puncture. A few more checks throughout the evening and he was still favoring that eye. I found him

Sebastian loves to go out into the hallway of our building and keep a watchful eye on the door to our apartment exercising his independence.

on my bed curled up next to the pillow in the dark. Sidney soon took up residence on the bottom of the bed, so as to keep him company. It appeared she was concerned about him, too. Otherwise she would have been with me in the office.

Sebastian chose the loveseat to camp out on when I went to bed. I lay there worried about him. I know, I'll say a prayer over him and ask Jesus and the angels to repair his eye during the night. I walked into the living room in the dark and knelt down by Sebastian with one hand around his hind end and the other on his head.

"Dear Jesus, please send your angels to heal Sebastian's eye tonight so I won't have to take him to the vet. Thank you, Jesus. In the name of Jesus Christ, our Lord, Amen."

The next morning, Sebastian was up and acting just as normal as can be. Paying particular attention to his eye all appeared to be fine. "Thank you, Jesus." I prayed. He cares about the animals, too.

Let Me Out!

The noise in the closet!

Cats hate a closed door, you know,
regardless of which side they're on.
If they're out, they want to get in and
if they're in, they want to go out.

Lilian Jackson Braun

On this November afternoon, the wind was whistling and doing its best to blow the last of the fall colored leaves off of the branches that waved wildly outside my office window. I was typing at my laptop and paused long enough to get up and walk through the living room, grabbing my denim jacket and hanging it up in the closet. I needed to get up and stretch. With the office window opened a crack for ventilation I thought a wool scarf around my shoulders would cut the chill. It was quite brisk out as the forecast called for more light rain, blustery conditions and much cooler temperatures than what we had comfortably gotten used to. Winter was on its way.

Since it was late afternoon and I didn't have a light on in the living room, I flipped on the entry light overhead so I could spot my scarf. After hanging up my jacket, I pulled the scarf away from another coat, caught the hat that was resting on them and adjusted it so it would not fall and closed the door. Flipping off the light switch, I turned and went back to my computer.

Sidney was out of sight as was Sebastian which wasn't all that unusual. The wind outside hadn't really let up and kept those leaves fluttering so. Then I heard this noise that sounded like the flap of a vent. I figured it was the dryer vent. Sometimes with the wind currents, such things do occur. I resumed my research pouring over some textbooks I'd picked up at the local library for my book. The material at hand was quite interesting and I found myself immersed in the pages and photos of my subject matter. There was that noise again. "That wind is really nasty out there" I thought as I continued reading, turning the pages and absorbing as much of the information as I could. I really didn't need to take notes as I was just fishing for tidbits to enhance and grow the length of my novel. That noise again was quite audible and wasn't all that familiar. I'd lived here for over four years now and had known of some pretty treacherous winds, but hadn't really heard the vents make that noise. Several minutes had passed now as I tried to accept it as just the residual effect of a strong wind current.

And then it was more of a clatter! So I arose to see what was the matter. (Sorry) I strode through the darkened living room and came around to the closet in the entryway. Clatter, clatter went the sound. WHAT was that all about? It surely wasn't a mouse this time. It was coming from inside the closet! I opened the door and out came Sebastian. Apparently, when I opened the door of the closet to retrieve my scarf, he decided to check things out with his unofficial snooper's license. He was so quick.

"Oh my gosh!" I exclaimed. "I'm SO sorry, Sebastian." He was in the closet long enough to have checked things out and then to determine that it wasn't fun anymore and wanted to get out--now! Poor thing.

In the past, this scenario had been played out more than once— with both Sebastian and then Sidney. I forget that when a door opens that is not ordinarily opened, they have to go in and check it out. It's an automatic invitation. It's also in their nature to 'hunt' and see what's there. And I don't always think to take a 'cat-count' before closing the door when I'm finished getting whatever it is I need out of there. Then, I'll either hear a scratching or a muffled meowing. But in this case, Sebastian didn't meow. Or if he did, I didn't hear him. I'd had the television on also but usually I have a keen ear about such things, especially when it involves either one of them.

Before I closed the door, I quickly sniffed to see if I could sense any remembrances but alas, he was very discreet and didn't leave any. He was, however, extremely happy to be OUT of there! He didn't warm up to me to show his appreciation. I think he was a little miffed that I hadn't acknowledged the noises earlier. If I were in his paws, I'd probably act the same way.

I think the longest I had left either of them in a closed room was maybe an hour. Today marked that hour. I felt badly and gave him a stroke or two as he wasn't any too anxious to greet me. 'How could you, Mom?' He probably thought. And I don't blame him.

This had happened before. Next time, I would have to be sure to do a 'cat-count' before I closed any doors inside the apartment.

Priceless

Love at what cost?

*The protein in a cats' saliva
causes the allergies.*

"No smoking cat hair." The doctor smugly advised as he tore off the script and handed it to me. We'd been through this same thing before. Same script, same directives. I was putting off having to go in to see him anyway because the sinus that was playing havoc with my quality of life was getting the better of me. It really wasn't infected, just terribly annoying. It was going into my chest, disrupting my breathing and my sleep.

Now when one is deprived of the minimum amount of sleep to function, there are several consequences. One being your attention span is just not as sharp as it used to be. Another negative factor is that you tend to gain weight with the lack of sleep; the body doesn't have enough time to digest the foods consumed. And then your immune system weakens and if there's any kind of a 'bug' in the air, say, from a shopping cart, a door knob, and you either rub your eye or pick your chapped lip and bingo. Guilty.

Only this time, the cat dandruff and loose hair was the culprit. And the doctor knew it.

"Get rid of the cats." He advised delivering his verdict.

I felt as though someone had knocked the air out of me. I wanted to use a word picture on the doc so he could know how I felt about this sentence. 'Ok, doc. Cut off your right arm. Oh! Isn't that the one you use to write your scripts? Ummmm, too bad. It's gotta go.' Or, come back with this one, 'hey doc, you have four boys, right? Which two would you give away? You'd still have two to carry on the family name'. I thought with my chin dragging on the elevator floor as I descended to the first floor. I turned down the long hall that took me into the adjoining building and on to the x-ray department. I thought that with all of the sinus problems I had encountered through the years that maybe there was an obstruction that I could blame my problems on. I honestly knew better but I needed a scapegoat.

When I got to the counter to be registered, the lady there was very empathetic and was quick to comfort me by telling me her story. Her husband had been allergic to their cats and they'd had the cats for several years. They had three and whenever he came home from work, he would quickly ruffle the tops of their heads and keep on walking. The kind lady went on to explain how she vacuums frequently and bathes them every few weeks. That would keep them from shedding as they love to lay in the sun drying out their skin. Made sense. But the last time I tried to bathe Sebastian, he fought me so. With his hind paws still intact, the claws came out and left nice holes in the shirt I was wearing. I finally took both of them into the pet store and an attendant there gave them baths. Sebastian wasn't too excited but Sidney loved the massage and toweling down to dry.

I really appreciated the lady's' story as it boosted my spirits and gave me the reassurance I needed knowing that if I just tried some alternative methods of cleaning both the apartment and the cats that I might survive and maintain my position of pet owner. I surely felt better after having talked to her. God had placed her in my path that day and gave me just the right words I needed to hear.

Two x-rays later and the doctor apparently didn't find anything wrong. He never brought it up and I kept forgetting to ask him about them. I'm sure if there was anything notable, he would have mentioned it.

A trip to the local hardware store and I picked up an air purifier that looked like a space vehicle on a launch pad. Hey! As long as it did the job, I really didn't care what it looked like as long as it had a Hepa filter I was good to go. I set that up and within a short time I could tell the difference. This air purifier was much larger than the one I had in the bedroom. I quickly read the instructions and for some reason I understood the filter would be good for a year. About two months later, I began to fill up with chest congestion again. I checked the air purifier instruction book. Depending on its use, I was to change the filter more often. Oh, to be able to read! Immediately I changed out the filter, which needed changing badly, and I was good to go again. So now, I have my own personal maintenance regimen down so I can keep the visits to the doc at a minimum.

Two prescription medications from the doctor	$57.00
Cough medication for chest congestion	$ 8.97
Office visit (after insurance)	$73.00
Air purifier with Hepa filter	$249.00
Unconditional love from two loving cats—	
lowering my blood pressure, cholesterol	
and triglycerides and reducing the risk	
of getting cancer. AND if I had a heart attack,	
I would heal quicker.	***Priceless***

I won't ask you to decide on the outcome. The cats stay. Period. Paragraph. Finito! Over and out! End of discussion.

In defense of cat ownership, allow me to explain the advantages:

Cats are extremely independent which means you don't have to cater to them. They are pretty simple to maintain and care for. You don't have to walk them. Just have food, water and a nice comfy surface or two for them to curl up on and they are happy and contented as can be. Having a shelf or a chair at the window is most helpful as cats love to look outside and observe the trees, leaves, birds, people, or anything else that moves.

You don't necessarily have to bathe them. They clean themselves. Dogs don't. Dogs smell after a while and need to be bathed. Not a cat!

Cats bring personal blessings of comfort and companionship.

There are many health benefits too. They can lower your blood pressure. When you pet a purring cat, you not only soothe the cat but generate and contribute something positive to your own health. Oxytocin is released which is a hormonal exchange between cat and human.

Cats are discerning and intelligent. They remember where they live. Cats have been known to have taken off for months or years from a residence and somehow have found their way home or to their owner. Okay, not so in my case but nevertheless I still got him back thanks to many angels along the way. There's power in prayer and there are people out there who care.

Most cats are affectionate and will either curl up next to you or be so bold as to walk onto your lap and make themselves comfortable. They have this need to be petted and loved and seem to sense when you are not feeling well or are sad and will comfort you as only a cat can. One time I was having a boo-hoo moment with another pet cat years ago and my cat actually came up to me and placed one paw on my thigh and the other on my cheek as if to wipe a tear. It was so touching and endearing.

Cats are curious creatures and can be extremely helpful if you have another critter in your midst. They will do their darndest to seek out the disturbance and bring it out of wherever it is hiding and bring judgment onto the intruder. Be it a fly, a mouse, a bee, or other species other than themselves. They will find these extremely entertaining and will play with them for some time before devouring them. Sidney has digested flies and almost a wasp. (Thank heavens I discovered it on the rug before she got serious about her intentions!) And the mouse? They will play with it for hours and wear themselves and the mouse out before they will let go of the hunt. We would do well to fashion and nurture our own sense of curiosity to maintain the child inside all of us. It could extend our lives; we would never grow 'old.'

Cats will evaluate a situation before approaching it. They operate with caution rather than emotion or fear. We could learn something from them in this aspect, also.

Cats remind us that playtime is every bit as important as work time. They will sprint after something just to playfully sprint at some-

Here are my precious babes; Sebastian and Sidney. They are a team; my 'healers of the heart.' You can see they enjoy one another's company and actually like one another

thing. It takes the innocence of a kitten at play to help you realize that even though things may be going badly in your life that it's important to 'lighten up.' Allow a kitten at play to remind you to let go of your fears and laugh a little. Let them bless you with a smile and assurance that everything will be okay. After all, God is in control.

Cats have also reduced the number of headaches among cat owners as well as bouts of fever and indigestion and cases of insomnia. Cat owners have also displayed lower levels of risk factors for cardiovascular disease. Being a cat owner has also shown to increase a patient's survival rate following a hospital stay for heart problems. Also, a human with a cat will recover more quickly from surgery or illness and deal better with stressful situations.

Cats can give us a positive sense of optimism and can help us feel less lonely and depressed. Having a cat as a pet can help one feel less isolated from other humans. They offer us unconditional love and what a blessing that is.

Cats show us it's okay to take a break and take a nap.

Cats show us how to be individuals, trusting in our own instincts, being happy with who we are and trusting our own inner voice.

Animal shelters are overflowing with all kinds, sizes, colors and numbers of wonderful feline friends just waiting for you to take them home and curl up with. Check out the Yellow Pages.

There's a Mouse in the House
Two against One

> *When I would read my stories to the writing*
> *group, it tickled me to see businessmen soften,*
> *smile and lighten up at my cats' antics.*
>
> **K. Clark**

It was early evening and I was watching the news on TV. All of a sudden I heard this awfully loud racket from the laundry room. The door was closed, thank heavens, so whatever it was, it was confined. I slowly got up off the couch and went over to the door, opening it slowly. There it was again and it appeared to be in the dryer vent. Whatever animal was there, it was huge by the level of noise. I carefully closed the door and went to my front door and knocked on the neighbor's door.

"Ah, Chris?" I inquired as I stood there with wide eyes and this look of fright on my face.

"Ya!" Chris and his wife, Erika, are very good neighbors and are very helpful in times of need or concern. This was a big concern at the moment.

"Could you check my laundry room out? There's something in there that's making a lot of noise!"

"Oh sure." And he came across the hall, into my apartment unit and over by the laundry room door. He opened the door and looked in on the vent.

"Whatever it is, it's in the dryer vent." I told him. There was that horrific noise again. "It's probably a mouse." Chris offered.

The dryer vent was one of those accordion shaped silver foil round funnels that transported the lint from the clothes out thru the vent and outside. Chris then proceeded to pull the dryer out from the wall dislodging the vent from the machine. We discovered a large amount of lint that had fallen out of the vent and found a pair of work gloves also. Chris shook the vent a little and there was nothing there. Somehow he reattached the vent tubing and pushed the dryer almost all the way to the wall. Which was ok. It needed a good cleaning.

"Wow!" "With all of that lint, I should have a professional come and clean that out." I exclaimed at the sight of all of that potentially hazardous material.

"That could be a fire hazard!" I added.

"I know of a fellow who cleans dryer vents. He lives out in this one village. I'll get you his name and number for you." Chris offered.

Chris was most helpful and knew a lot of people in his line of work. He was the managing editor of a small newspaper and had a lot of contacts. He invited me to be a reporter for the newspaper also, which I really enjoyed doing. I was grateful for any help he could lend me.

"It's probably just a mouse." Chris suggested again.

"Oh, great! Just what the cats need."

Chris' job was done so he left and went back to his apartment. At least that took care of the noise in the laundry room. I looked up the name and number of the fellow who would be cleaning the vent and would give him a call tomorrow since the day was just about over.

All was quiet for a while and I was back watching a movie on TV. It was about nine o'clock in the evening and all of a sudden Sidney was causing a raucous in the bathroom. I know she can get excited over the silliest items. Given something as simple as a rubber band or even that ring around the plastic milk carton. However, she was doing some serious wrestling with something. Soon, she came out of the bathroom with this teeny tiny baby mouse in her mouth.

"Oh my gosh, Sidney!" She dropped it and it scooted off under the loveseat. 'Oh dear,' I thought. I didn't have a trap and then I didn't want to endanger the cats with that, either. I know they like to catch their prey and then drop it at your feet to 'show and tell'. This is their way of showing you their appreciation of your taking care of them and letting you know of their hunting prowess. I was tired but I wasn't going to bed only to have a mouse dropped on my comforter only to scamper under the sheets! Instead I decided I would just let them play with it until everyone tired themselves out. What other option did I have? I wasn't going anywhere.

I kind of felt sorry for the little guy. I mean, here were two huge monsters with these huge eyes and paws coming after it, swiping and chasing it here and there. He got under the loveseat with Sidney on one side and Sebastian on the other. It didn't take Sebastian long to figure out what all the fuss was about and he quickly joined in the chase and frolic.

In the meantime, I curled my legs up under me. I wasn't going to have this little creature run over my feet. Pretty soon the little guy came through the living room in front of the TV and around by the stereo with Sidney right behind. Sidney outstretched a paw in hopes of softly batting it so she could play with it but the little trooper waddled too fast for him over the woven carpet. Under the couch he went. The way the little twerp was navigating the threads of the carpet besides being scared out of his wits, he wasn't making much headway but somehow just seemed to remain out of reach of my monsters.

It was 12:45 a.m. The movie was over. I was tired. And the cats had curled up on the couches tired from all of the excitement. I figured the baby mouse must have found refuge behind my bookcase near the front door. So I went to bed satisfied that things had settled down. Hopefully there wouldn't be any more activity throughout the rest of the night.

When I came through the living room the next day, there was the baby mouse in the middle of the living room in front of the TV. He was on his back with all fours up in the air. Was he playing dead or was he still exhausted from last night's chase?

"Oh Sidney, look! Here's your little buddy." I said alerting and inviting Sidney to continue her play with the tiny rodent in hopes of ending this exciting pursuit. Upon closer inspection, the little fella was still on his back with all fours up in the air. Sidney came over and bat

Yes, this is a REAL mouse and it kept them busy for a few hours one evening until they all exhausted themselves. The mouse was tossed over the patio deck the next day

ted it and the tiny mouse moved ever so slowly as if to surrender to any activity or life that he might have hoped for.

Ok, that's it. Game over. I went into the pantry and grabbed one of the work gloves, went over to the tiny mouse and picked it up by it's tail. He didn't fight it. Then I opened the sliding glass door to the patio, went out and gave him a big heave. Done. End of play time.

A few days later and Sidney was still looking in corners hoping to find her little buddy. But no playmate was to be found. Mom called the game. Everything and everyone was intact. And we're on the second floor!

"You Come Here Often?"
What's Your Sign?

If you want to know the character of a man,
find out what his cat thinks of him.

Anonymous

In front of my bedroom window are two surfaces meant for observation; one is a bar stool that is just the right height and the other is a cat condo with a flat top quite suitable for perching and viewing the world outside. On occasion, when either one, but especially Sebastian, is perched on the stool at night, I will come over, lean in and fold my arms on the other perch. Just to make conversation, I'll start with…

"So-a, you come here often?" and I will turn to him expecting him to tell me or at least acknowledge me, both of which he never does. He has such an adorable profile I have to forgive him.

"What's your Sign?" I follow up with my conversation starter but, again, he's so engrossed in taking in any activity down below that I'm part of the woodwork.

In my research, I found that there are pet astrological signs. I mean, why not. They were born in a certain month. So I looked it up on the Internet.

Sebastian is a Cancer. Here's what www.pethoroscopesgo.com/pet-signs.shtml had to say about Cancer cats:

If you're looking for a loyal animal that's totally committed to your home and your family, you're going to want a Cancer pet. They aren't the type to stray too far from your house, and they would definitely be great cats, because they are very protective."

I don't know what to say. "They aren't the type to stray…." Ok, let's just dismiss this as a generality. But then when I had another reading done, I was told, and this one was much more legitimate, that he had every intention of running away. When I look back now, I can understand this. Let's find out more about the Cancer Cat = Sebastian.

According to Anna Lynn Sibal, "A Cancer Cat that keeps an entire neighborhood awake all night with his loud mewing and cater-wauling, as if he is singing to the moon, is more than likely to be a Cancer Cat. That is because the Cancer cat loves the sound of his voice so much that he will even meow in turn to his favorite song when it is played on the radio. He will even sing his purring song while chilling on his owner's lap."

When Sebastian took off, I don't know and can't say that he wailed at the moon or kept the neighbors up and I've observed that when I let him out for a short romp he likes the sound of his own voice and will announce his presence to the neighborhood. He will also let himself be known if he wants something and that's to be expected. I've never heard him sing along with the radio while on my lap. That said, let's see what else are some of the other characteristics:

"Laps are where one will almost always find a Cancer Cat. Cancer Cats are perfect lap cats. They can stay there, still and content, for hours on end. A lot of times, a Cancer cat looks so peaceful on one's lap that it is sheer rudeness to dislodge him from his repose."

Sebastian will walk right over to my lap and make himself at home and will be quite content. For hours? I don't think so, but nevertheless, a good amount of time. And I've learned that when cats are sleeping or in this case peacefully lounging on your lap, it is rude to upset them so I go with his flow. He'll make himself quite comfortable and loves to be cuddled and petted, of course. That's when I call him my 'sweetheart'. He melts my heart.

"A Cancer Cat is also often found asleep most of the day. That's because he is generally a nocturnal cat, a creature of the night. It is hard to rouse him and keep him awake during the daytime but come nighttime, he is at his most alert and awake. He would run around with his friend across the neighborhood's rooftops, singing to the top of his voice and hunting."

Yes, Sebastian is definitely a sleeper a good part of the day and he and Sidney will race around here at night when I'm trying to settle down. Ah-as far as running across rooftops, not this one. He stays in at night. I know a favorite comment at night when the family closes up the house is to ask, "Did you let the cat out?" That doesn't happen here. For one, his roaming days are over. Especially in the city. There's way too much traffic to feel safe with him running wild out there and another, there are a lot of other critters running loose. I will see road kill of all kinds and even on my trek home, I will see wild animals scurry out of the way. So for Sebastian's own protection, I keep him in at night. It's just a good idea. Besides, if he were to be injured, the vet bill around here could be quite expensive.

"Noisy that he is, a Cancer Cat rarely gets into trouble. He never gets into fights with other cats because he is quite a timid cat. He shies away from fights and conflicts the moment he smells it. It is not because he is a scaredy-cat; it is more because of his shy and peaceful nature. But when the Cancer Cat is cornered, he definitely snaps and fights back."

Ok, so maybe Sebastian is timid when it comes to critter confrontation. Whenever I've taken him out to the park just north of us in the daytime, I've never seen him have to deal with another animal, so I don't know how he would react. I keep a pretty close eye on him. I'm sure he would scamper as fast as he could, though. I do remember, when we visited his 'mom' on the farm after that first year, I was visiting with Kathy and all of a sudden, we saw Sebastian racing from around the front of the house to the back and being chased by none other than his Mother! Sebastian was pouring it on as he raced across the drive and behind a building. I hope he escaped her clutches. It wasn't long and I had him back in the car. Wouldn't you have thought his birth Mother would have recognized him and made up to him? Apparently not. Not in this case. Maybe she felt he was now an intruder trying to come back into her territory. At any rate, I was quite surprised by this behavior.

"Inasmuch as a Cancer cat tries to get as far away from trouble as

he could, he loves being the center of loving attention. He can be a real feline prince. He loves to be coddled and pampered; this is actually why he loves laps. Ignore him and he becomes moody and sulky. If he is scolded for anything, he whines and meows piteously and mopes around the house until his owner scoops him up and lets him on her lap again."

Oh yes, Sebastian loves to be the center of loving attention. And yes, he can be a real prince and loves to be coddled and pampered. I read somewhere where you're nobody until you've been ignored by a cat. But if you ignore Sebastian he has been known to sulk. He will curl up either on my bed in the darkened room, on the loveseat or in the cradle in the darkened office and almost hide his face as if in a sulk. On occasion I have had to scold him and sometimes he will take it out on Sidney. He knows when he's done something I'm not pleased with. Such as picking on Sidney when she's lying there completely innocent. He may have remembered a time or two when Sidney sauntered up next to me, wound herself around and plopped up against my thigh. She loves to have here ears massaged. I do believe he gets jealous. I have to get after him as she does not deserve an unprovoked attack.

"The Cancer Cat is vulnerable to throat problems this year, especially when the autumn season comes. His owner should try to keep him indoors when the cold months come."

I guess I've been forewarned. I don't generally let him out in the cold winter months. If I did, it would only be out on the patio where he could get a taste of the cold air, check out any other scents, take attendance of any little critters scampering on the ground or checking out the birds only to quickly pivot and come back in again. At least he would know why he's being kept inside.

"Gastric problems may also bother the Cancer Cat this year. He loves eating, especially the tastier types of tidbits, but he should not be allowed to eat more than he should."

I've noticed he has appeared thinner than maybe a year ago. But I also noticed he had one of his large teeth missing. Maybe it was and is still somewhat tender there so he doesn't eat as much. It may just be his metabolism also that keeps him trim. He seems to be satisfied to pick as cats have been known to make at least some twenty trips to their cat dishes in a day.

"If his owner wants to teach her Cancer Cat a few kitty tricks, this year is the time to do it, as the intelligent Cancer Cat would be more receptive to any instruction right now more than ever."

Interesting! Shall we introduce potty training?

"Another thing that this year may hold for the beautiful Cancer Cat prince is the possibility of kittens. He might take it upon himself to chase after the tomcats, and the tomcats will not be able to resist him. The household that the Cancer Cat lives in should prepare for his litter."

Ok, I changed the gender of the prediction to fit Sebastian and since he's been fixed, this eliminates any and all of the above. And as far as any tomcats, I don't believe he's gay.

Sidney is a Gemini. Born May 26, 2009 to be exact. (Same as my ex.)

Lynn Lopez writes about Pet Astrological Signs on the Internet and says,

"A pet's astrological sign can help owners learn more about the animal's temperament, but don't let that dictate your pet-buying or choosing decision. Any pet, regardless of its astrological sign, deserves a good home, a human that will take care of it, and plenty of food, love and affection."

Turns out, I picked out the cats before I even considered or thought of their astrological signs. However, I have made note that the characteristics listed here pretty well match their personalities and temperaments. Who would have thought?

"The Gemini Cat falls under the sign of the Twins and are said to be very vocal and expressive, so a Gemini pet may tend to meow a lot. They are also quite restless and crave a lot of new activities, so don't forget to keep them entertained by introducing variety in their everyday lives."

Sidney is definitely very vocal. If you recall, her original mother even took her to the vet to find out if all that "conversation" was normal. The vet quite assuredly told her that she was fine. She just liked to 'talk' a lot. She is definitely more active than Sebastian and playful. She will be the first to spontaneously race through the apartment and crouch and jump at Sebastian in play.

In another description of Gemini's (not necessarily cats), it described them as "adaptable, versatile, communicative, witty, youthful, lively, nervous, tense, cunning and inquisitive."

Sidney was certainly adaptable. She came from a home of ten cats and then coming to live with just me and now Sebastian, I believe she has done quite well. She can be restless and doesn't sleep as much as Sebastian. She has explored many different places to nap and enjoys crawling into small places. Maybe it's a security thing. I think she enjoys the one-on-one or one-on-two environment. Her original mother told me she would lay near her head or chest at night so she likes to cuddle and feel close to a human also. Lively and inquisitive? Oh definitely. She will be the one to stick her head into an open cabinet or check out the storage closet. Sometimes I'll leave the laundry room door open with the light out. I'll catch the back end of Sidney cautiously and ever so quietly checking it out with her "Snooper's License" in tow.

Anna Lynn Sibal has this to say about Gemini Cats: *"The Gemini Cat is an angel among domestic felines. She is remarkably obedient, more so than is usual among others of her species. A sensitive, perhaps even emphatic cat, it may seem that she can actually understand what is being said to her, to the point that she may sometimes meow back in response. She is a very charming creature, and she will keep her owners entertained with her antics for hours on end."*

Despite the fact that she is inquisitive, she is an angel. Sidney has such a quiet unassuming demeanor. And charming? Oh, indeed. When I call her name, she is quick to respond and will come to me when called. Maybe not right off, but eventually. Before I settle down in bed in the evening, she will hunker down under a chair I have in the bedroom and we will carry on a conversation. I think she thinks I'm trying to persuade her to join me and we'll banter back and forth until she has convinced me that she's quite content where she is. And then other evenings she will be more than happy to join me. Sidney is definitely entertaining with her antics. One doesn't have to spend a lot or anything on elaborate 'toys' to entertain her. She is quite satisfied playing with the simplest things around the apartment.

"As placid as the Gemini Cat's disposition may be, the Gemini Cat nonetheless has a nose for trouble. She is a very curious soul; it can be claimed that the saying "Curiosity killed the cat" was coined especially for her, because certainly her curiosity can get her into a lot of scrapes than her owner could count. It could be tumbling into a bowl of cream that her owner forgot to put away. It could be chasing another cat through the neighbor's meticulously cared-for flowerbed. It could be anything."

Sidney, it would seem, can never get enough food. I brought home leftovers from a dinner out that included chicken. I thought I had pretty well cleaned off the bones and gathered them up in a couple of paper napkins and tossed them in the garbage receptacle. Later on I emptied the garbage from the container and tied the ties on the bag and put them in the front hallway just inside the door. Wrong move. It wasn't long and Sidney discovered the chicken aroma. She carefully picked at the plastic, pulled out the napkins and bones and began chewing on them. Chicken bones can be extremely hazardous to animals if they get them lodged in their throats. I re-bagged it, doubling my efforts to conceal the goodies. This was no deterrent so the next morning, the garbage went out and down to the dumpsters.

Sidney will often times be the one to instigate a chase. I'm minus one teapot for evidence. It got in the way of a serious rumble between her and Sebastian.

"The Gemini Cat also loves to hunt, simply for the joy of hunting. Her prey could be a mouse, someone's pet hamster, a goldfish or that unlucky sparrow that happened to perch on the windowsill without noticing her. She will never eat her prey once she has caught it, though. What she will do, is to lay it on the feet of her owner, like some kind of offering."

Sidney doesn't go outside. Having been raised as an indoor cat, an indoor cat is what she will be. A hunter out in the wild she will never be. She will, however, play with a mouse and bat it around for quite some time to the point of tiring herself (and the mouse) out. Such as the case when there was one loose in our apartment from the dryer vent. And no, she didn't eat the mouse--just spent hours terrifying the tiny creature. That's why I let all three of them; Sebastian, Sidney and the mouse, tire one another out one evening.

Above the sliding glass doors are three vents, one of which has been home to numerous black bird nests through the years. I let the cats out on the deck and within a short time there was a scuffle and I heard a loud chirp from the rocking chair I have set out there. Mind you, this is near midnight. I got up from my chair and I went to the opened door where I saw Sidney making her way towards the opening with a large bird in her mouth. The front half of her body made it through the door before I closed it on her dislodging the terrified bird. "Sorry, Sidney but only cats are allowed in here." The bird stumbled across the deck and made it to the railing before Sebastian could swatch him. He appeared to be stuck, but soon tumbled over the edge. The bird was much smaller than I first noticed as his wing span almost covered Sidney's face. Maybe the bird fell out of the nest, I didn't know why he was on the deck so late in the evening. What would I have done with a live bird in the apartment at that time of the evening?

"The Gemini Cat is also a prankster. Her owner should not really be surprised should the Gemini Cat just jump on her shoulder out of nowhere. She is not really fond of cuddling either, so her owner should never force her to sit on her lap if she does not want to."

THAT'S my Sidney! She will cuddle but will not get up on my lap. And I don't force her to. Sebastian is just the opposite. He will get in all the cuddling he can handle and he's on my lap at least once a day and for some time. It appears he needs his daily dose of affection from Mom. And, of course, Mom could use some, too. I thought that Sidney's lack of this sign of affection unusual having coming from a home of ten other cats. I thought she would have welcomed the one-on-one cuddle and lap time. But not Sidney. She is a true Gemini in this respect.

"This summer may find the Gemini Cat in a sociable mood. She is usually friendly with other pets, but she would seem to be even friendlier during this season. It would not be unusual to find tomcats prowling around the lovely Gemini-girl-cat and serenading her at night. It may count for a lot of sleepless nights this summer, but the Gemini cat may appear to be quite happy about it. Perhaps a litter of kittens can be expected soon afterwards."

This would not be Sidney this summer or the next. She has been fixed and not allowed outside. I know their sense of smell is acute, but I have not heard of nor seen any other cats under the bedroom window serenading her which is fine with me and I'm sure, the other neighbor's. No kittens in this nest, thank you.

"The coolness of autumn may make the Gemini Cat appear to wane in her affections as well, but it could only mean that she is becoming a little restless. If she snarls at her owner, her owner should not take it personally and should just leave her alone. If she wants to go out, she should be let out, lest she take her aggression and restlessness on furniture legs and rugs. She could also be craving for some nice tidbits, and she should be indulged every once in awhile."

One evening I was rubbing her tummy and neck and she appeared to be loving it. However, all of a sudden, she let out a "hiss" at me, so I stopped. I hadn't observed her being restless and since she's been fixed I believe that has taken care of the situation. She does like her occasional treat, however.

"When the winter comes, all that restlessness would go away and she would even be more affectionate than she usually is. The normally adventurous and trouble-seeking Gemini feline may actually seek her owner's lap and stay there for as long as she can. Winter is also a good time to introduce new pets with the Gemini Cat. She would be more welcoming of them by then."

Winter can be quiet around here and I would be surprised if she sought out my lap. And just for the record, no other animals will be introduced to this environment, thank you.

A Lazy Afternoon
Another day in Paradise ??

There is no snooze button on a cat who wants breakfast.

Unknown

It's Wednesday afternoon in November and the kitties are doing well. Both napping as usual. In that respect they are NOT good role models. It's too easy to join them when I have so many other things to do. Housekeeping for one. No, it's not one of my favorites. To look around this place you'd think that this was the cats' apartment and I just slept here and paid the rent. You know those plastic rings around milk cartons? Sidney loves to play with those. And the rubber bands the mail lady wraps around your advertisements? Sidney loves to play with those also. I know, rubber bands are one of the items on the list of things that your cat shouldn't play with, but she just bites them and carries them from room to room. I think she's fascinated with the texture. At any rate, those two items are numerous and scattered all over the bedroom, living room and office floors along with other cat toys.

There are only three large rooms in this apartment, but four doors that could be closed. I keep them open so the kitties can snoop around. They love to investigate and check everything out with their noses sniffing here and there. They come with unofficial "Snooper's Licenses." Two of the rooms are closets with boxes and neat things to investigate and hide behind or climb up on to and see how high they can go. I'll bet they would be very good at doing inventory around here. Too bad they can't verbally express themselves so I could easily understand them.

"Sidney, do you know where the box of CDs are that I packed away last fall?"

"Ya, Ma, they're in the spare room closet on the floor under your box of gifts."

"Oh, thank you. I wondered where I hid them."

What a wonderful thing that would be to have someone else to keep track of my stuff. I have limited space here, (compared to the room I left at my home in Bartlett), and really don't like to put things in boxes that I'm not using. They only take up space. But you can't use all of your stuff all of the time. And the cats would tell me these things in the nicest way. None of that, "Your crap is in the other room."

They love it when I open the windows a bit. The view is their window on their world. Since their sense of smell is so acute, they love to smell the different aromas from the outside. They can detect animals, people, cars, trees, plants, etc. All of these scents are a delight to capture the attention of if only for a few moments until they're satisfied. And they love to 'take attendance' to see who's out and about. Since their eyes are so keen they can spot anything that moves. And that includes those four legged little critters, the mouse. Or an occasional squirrel. But the mouse is the most fascinating.

One day, Sebastian found one while I was taking out the garbage. Poor little mouse. There were some bushes alongside this one building and on the ground where the leaves had gathered, a little mouse was trying his best to hide from this whiskered, four legged monster with the huge paws. This tiny mouse was trying his best to play dead so Sebastian would ignore him. But then Sebastian would cuff him around to arouse him and found he was still alive. The mouse would try to scamper as best he could to get out of his reach, but Sebastian was right there ready to cuff him around again with his extended paw. That poor little mouse must have been terrified. Then I saw Sebastian pawing him around in the dirt. The neighbors from another building came out and saw all of this happening, finding it entertaining and said, "Hi Sebastian!" Apparently they knew him. (!)

Sebastian had a fan club going on that I wasn't aware of. I didn't know these people. He is charming, cute and friendly. I'm sure if you saw him, you would want to pet him, too. He's much friendlier than

Sidney. I finally got Sebastian's attention, picked him up and we headed back toward our building. I was wondering if the mouse was able to revive himself enough to seek safe shelter. Hopefully he recovered from his frightening experience from that furry neighborhood bully, aka, Sebastian.

It's a little later on in the day and they are both snoozing once again. Sebastian is curled up on the couch in the living room and Sidney is on the rocking chair huddled down on the blanket in the office. What a cat's life. Makes me want to cave in and curl up, too.

Earlier, Sebastian was following the sun as it radiated through the bedroom window and on the carpet. He loves to sprawl out and enjoy the heat from it. At one point he was in front of the sliding glass door curled up in one of the three cloth cubes that I have there with the open holes on three sides. Once in a while they'll race through them chasing one another. In the meantime, Sidney was laying outside of the cubes and on the carpet close to him. She loves the sun, also.

It's been a rather quiet day at our abode. The sun is quickly descending the western sky. It seems when it's just rising or setting, it moves the fastest. Every second counts where the sun's light is concerned in a cat's life. In a matter of moments the landscape changes so, either brightening or darkening until the street lights, or in this case, the parking lot lights, pop on. Then it's time to find the living room couches once again and be near "Mom" as we all sometimes watch TV. Then it's nap time again until she turns off the lights.

Ok, I finally caved. The peepers slammed shut as I let my head drop down on my folded arms that satisfied the comfort of a makeshift pillow. Even with the light on over the table, I still managed to shut that out and grab a few z's. It was only a tease, though. Sidney is still asleep in the rocking chair while Sebastian is in the living room. The window is open a little over an inch allowing the fresh fall air to cleanse and renew the atmosphere in here. No hint of pine as it's getting to be that time of the year. It's Thanksgiving Eve and all is quiet in the neighborhood. People are still en route home. Maybe they got off work early and are at the grocery store picking up those last minute

Sidney pretty well fills up the rocking chair!

items for the big feast tomorrow.

A Walk in the Preserve
Fun with Sebastian

*The cat could very well be man's best friend
but would never stoop to admitting it.*

Doug Larson

There had finally been a break in the temperatures as it was almost like a spring day outside. Sebastian and I had been hibernating of sorts in the air conditioning and it was time to stretch our legs and check out the Preserve just north of us.

I thought I'd best carry him until we got to the paved path on the west side of the complex and going into the Preserve. I had to cross a main road which was a large curve through the complex and go through a couple of parking lots and didn't want to take any chances. Even though the speed limit was fifteen miles an hour, I myself, rarely went that slow. After we cleared any possible hazards, I put him down and he knew where to go. If there's a path or sidewalk, he'll opt for the smoother surface.

The skies were absolutely beautiful. A deep blue with a few puffs of cotton ball-like clouds and just a hint of a breeze. The sun was warm but not intense. The storm from the night before cleared out the humidity but we needed the rain badly. Lawns and gardens were drying up. To conserve water, the city had asked that you temper your use of water to every other day. The trees and brush still appeared a little parched but a little more lively.

I like to steer off the paved path and take the wide grassy one that had been cleared and leads around the pond. There's just something relaxing and comforting to see a body of water.

Today there would even be a few ducks that picked up on our

rustle through the grass and paddled their way to the center and then to the other side of the man-made pond. They left small folds of water that branched out into a "V" formation as they fled across the cool waters. There was mama and her four little ducklings. They quacked to alert the others that there were visitors in their midst.

A few white and yellow butterflies darted here and there from the tops of weeds along the edge of the pond. Upon further investigation you could see the algae and moss that gathered around the sprigs of grass that were anchored in the shallow lake. There was the occasional bottle top wedged in the mud that you could easily see through the clear water.

On the left side of the path was a fence and then the preserve where cattails lived large and plenty. Red-winged blackbirds were precariously and often seen clinging to a branch until they decided their next move. And if you paid particular attention to the terrain you just might make out the head or two of some deer.

One evening on my trek in looking for Sebastian, I had my flashlight with me and to my left I heard a rustling of the weeds, shined my flashlight up on the hill and saw two eyes glowing back at me and the silhouette of the head and antlers of a deer. Not wanting to further disturb the wildlife that might be in the near vicinity, I decided to turn around and come back the next day. I'm not that brave.

On this particular day, Sebastian and I were just out enjoying the fresh air. With his sniffer in high gear, he checked out several places on our way past the pond. I would try to keep my stride and he would lag behind but then bolt to catch up. He was in his element and loving every minute of it.

We were headed toward the little, wooden, red bridge across a narrow spillway where the pond could flow into the preserve providing drink for the animals who were safely protected on the other side of the fence. It was a narrow walking bridge and we often stopped in the middle to check out anything that didn't quite make it through the rocks and sediment that gathered there. A dead fish could sometimes be seen, as maybe a plastic drinking cup. I always checked out the rungs of the railings for some perfect spider webs. As a camera buff, I get excited about them for an awesome photo. Not too keen on the spiders that might be lodged in them, but the webs, yes. Although a good close-up of a spider would be a pretty cool shot, too.

Sebastian, in the meantime, would be on either end of the bridge and wanting to check out the water flow. But the soft, wet soil kept him from venturing too far away from dry land. We would continue up the hill toward the hiking paths unless he chose to branch off and check out the thick growth of brush and weeds along the side of the pond. He had to check everything out which included what other animals had left there before him. The park and preserve were favorite places for people to walk their dogs. The parks department thoughtfully installed those containers with bags to pick up any dog droppings. Cats are much more discreet in this area. They carefully cover up their "gifts." And besides, who walks their cats?

I don't leash Sebastian as he pretty much stays close to me. And if he should stray, I just follow his lead and wait for him to finish his inspections. Then, after awhile he's ready to join in the excursion. We'll sometimes take a short walk on one of the trails. Again, he'll bolt ahead of me and slow down until I catch up and then he gets distracted either sniffing something out or watching a bug or checking out some other object left on the trail. One time he got way ahead of me and when he turned, he couldn't see me so he double-backed and checked me out to make sure I was still coming. He's so thoughtful that way. We're good companions for one another. Rarely complains.

After a short romp through the blades of grass, we'll start to head back. There's a picnic shelter after you get back from the paths and I like to sit there if Sebastian isn't ready to call it a day yet. Just when I think he'd be tired out, he's up and running inspecting another woodsy area across the parking lot that could harbor all kinds of little critters and then I have to go over and let him know I'm not far behind him. He likes to hide behind this blanket of brush and just hunker down and check out the surroundings. I think he thinks he's pulling one on me. I don't know. And it could be awhile before he decides he's had enough.

In the meantime, people have driven into the park and lined up along the edge and center of the lot either to go for an early evening stroll, walk their dogs or bring their children to play on the playground just beyond the parking lot. There are also benches strewn over the grounds so people can just sit and relax. There's another pond where the geese like to congregate and you might even find a father and young son along the edge dangling their fishing poles hoping for a bite or two. They really have it set up nicely and it's particularly beautiful after a fresh snow. The snow flocked trees have produced a few stunning winter shots for me.

When people bring their dogs, I have to approach them and get their attention warning them that there's a cat in the area. They need to know Sebastian's whereabouts knowing how keen a dogs' sense is. If the dog isn't leashed right away the dog could take off in Sebastian's direction and we'd be hard pressed to prevent some real harm to poor little Sebastian. Although, I believe Sebastian would put it in high gear and race out the other side of the area, heading for the playground or hopefully the paved path that heads home. Then I'd really be getting my exercise in trying to get him back! He may not be too eager to go to the park again.

On one particular visit to the park one day, as we headed home walking up the paved path, there was a couple with a stroller and a small babe. "Is that your cat?" They asked. Sebastian was following me fairly closely.

"Yes it is." I answered with pride. "That's my Sebastian."

They were quite impressed with the fact that he wasn't leashed and was following me home. To be honest, so was I but he did have it pretty good at home. He knew where he could be fed and loved.

On this particular walk, we veered off the paved path and on to this grassy knoll that brought us to one of the parking lots behind this one unit. Then we found the sidewalk and continued our trek home. A car had pulled into the lot and slowed to a stop. Inside was a young fellow and his passenger. At first they made hand jestures and pointed to Sebastian.

Shhhh.....All tuckered out. Guess that was a longer walk around the park than I realized. Sorry, Sebastian. Will you forgive me? Sebastian? OK, I'll leave you alone. Shhhhh.....

"Is that your cat?" they wanted to know.

"Yes, he's mine." Yet another couple who were impressed to see a cat out walking with it's owner--unleashed.

By the time we reached the front door of our building, a third person had taken notice and marveled at Sebastian following me knowing how independent cats can be. Sebastian just keeps endearing me with his actions and loyalty. Indeed, he is a special kitty to me and I continue to Thank God for allowing me to be his custodian.

"Rochester"
A Cat from another time

*If you yell at a cat, you're the
one making a fool of yourself.*

Unknown

I finally decided it was time for me to move out and take an apartment which was northwest of my parent's home in the same town. It was an older home and was made up of two apartments. I had the lower unit and eventually a friend moved upstairs for a short time. It was small but adequate and had a huge yard and a detached garage. Across the street were townspeople that I was familiar with. One was my science teacher from eighth grade and his family. Next door to them was a family of five; mom, dad, a little girl and twin boys about three years younger than she. The little girl with blonde hair came over often and we were fast friends. Laurie was very friendly.

The rental agreement said 'no pets.' However, this particular year the field mice went crazy propagating all over the place and since my back yard was next to a field, they were all over the place and soon found refuge in my little abode. First there was one, then two, then a third one and so on. Before the count was finished and the holes and openings covered, Rochester and I had seen fifteen of those little critters. Yes! And that was just one season.

After the first few invaders I began asking around if anyone knew of someone wanting to let go of a cat. I needed a good 'mouser.' A couple had referred me to some students who already had three cats and wanted to get rid of one, as they caused havoc racing all over their apartment. And being students, they were trying to cut down on expenses. The kitty cat was just adorable. All black with a white face, bib and four white paws.

Now I've learned that not all cats are good mousers. And as I recall, I believe Rochester only carried maybe one little guy outside in his mouth. The others he pretty much played with and batted around as a play toy. I would tend to favor giving kudos to my younger brother over Rochester as he nailed down several holes around the kitchen area and was much more helpful.

You may wonder how I came to name him Rochester? Remember Jack Benny's butler? (Jack Benny was a well-known comedian in the 50s, 60s and 70s). Since this kitty appeared to be wearing a tuxedo, I decided on Rochester. The name fit him so well. He strode around with such pride, dignity and such presence.

I remember when I took him over to my folks after I first picked him up, he just fit in the front of my ski jacket. He was so cute and adorable with just his little head popping out. I had a meeting scheduled that night but didn't go as I wanted to spend time with Rochester so we could bond. I didn't want to leave him alone the first night. It was more important we get to know one another and for him to become familiar with his new residence.

I don't recall Rochester being that friendly with me. I know he would jump up on the bottom of the bed sometimes, but he already had his nesting places picked out.

Ah, yes, I have many fond memories of Rochester...

There was an evening when I had a couple of student friends over and we were all sitting cross-legged on the floor when Rochester comes to the door. I'd left him outside to play, he knew his way back and would sometimes even jump up on the door handle to open it! Anyway, I let him in and in his mouth were bird feathers!

"Get out of here!" I scolded him exasperated with what I saw. He quickly turned around, exited the living room and went on outside.

I now know this is their way of showing you what a great hunters they are. They are so proud of their kill and they want to show you their appreciation. Needless to say, I wasn't at all impressed. Poor bird.

The science teacher across the street informed me that Rochester would terrorize his birds in his back yard. He had several bird houses and my neighbor didn't particularly appreciate Rochester's visits. Ok, so how do you keep your cat away from them when he's out and about? The science teacher also reported that he'd never seen a cat like Rochester. He went on to explain how Rochester would climb up a tree head first and come down the tree head first. A cat's claws are structured so that they have to back down the way they went up. But leave it to Rochester. And a science teacher should know. Some cats can get up a tree and then discover they don't know how to get down. Fortunately, I never had to call the fire department for an incident like this.

Before I would leave for work, I'd let him out and the neighbors would report back and delight in telling of his visits to their homes and yards.

There was the older lady who gardened in her back yard. Rochester would stop and visit with her a bit, dig in the dirt a little before going across the street and visiting another older lady who fed him hamburger and turkey. No wonder he didn't always come home when he could feast on her menu. All I offered him was cat food.

One afternoon I was laying on the couch and Rochester was laying behind a stand that had the TV on it. He began to make the sound of a trill, maybe it was a coo. So I returned the coo. Soon he was on my chest and we took turns cooing at one another as I petted him. We had connected.

When I came home from work late in the evening, I would park across the street. Immediately Rochester would come out from the neighbors hedge along the front of the house and make a dash for the car to join me and we walked into the house together.

"Well, hi there, Rochester. How are you?" I'd acknowledge him as he rubbed against my leg. We'd go into the house and when the weather was nice out, come right back out and take a walk around the block with him close beside me. It was nice to have a walking buddy.

One night on our walk, we were just a few houses from the apartment and we met up with one of the cats in the neighborhood. It was a calico and territorial. It was so dark out I really couldn't tell what exactly happened. I knew there was a skirmish between the two of them and one of them scampered up a maple tree. I wasn't sure if it was Rochester or not. I did hear a growl, apparently the other cat was close enough so the treed cat knew not to come down right away. I waited and waited. Finally, I thought I would just go home and eventually Rochester would come home. Well, he didn't come and didn't come. So I walked back to the tree and tried to coax him down. Eventually he came down and we returned home.

Then there was the evening he came back to the apartment and as he was sitting against the front door, I noticed he wasn't sitting squarely on the floor. It was as if he were favoring one side. I picked him up putting one hand under his chest and the other under his hind end. He moaned and squirmed. Ah-oh, I thought. Something's not right.

The next day I called the vet and made an appointment. Sure enough. He'd been in a cat fight and had an abscess. When the vet lanced it and pressed on it, this green goo came out as if it were from a toothpaste tube. Yuk! And Rochester was none too impressed either. The vet cleaned out the abscess, gave him a shot and soaked some gauze in medicine which he stuffed in to the infected area. Rochester had to be kept overnight.

When I went to pick him up, it appeared his eyeballs were circling their sockets as he was a little out of it. The pain killers were doing their job. I brought him home and placed him on this cushion on the wicker chair and knelt down on my knees to console and comfort him. He didn't care, and it wasn't long before he began pulling at the gauze. I guess that was a good sign as he didn't like it. I called the vet and he said he would be all right. Just keep him inside and keep an eye on him.

Another mouse memory: remember the little girl across the street? She came over one day and we were in the kitchen. All of a sudden a mouse came out from under the refrigerator and went under the wooden cabinets. We both let out a scream and jumped up on the chrome chairs. Then we heard a loud snap! And then this rattle. When

In one season, fifteen (15) mice!

we looked, we saw this tiny mouse with it's tail caught in the trap which had been the other side of the ledge of the cabinet. The mouse was visible on our side fighting for all he was worth to escape. Laurie and I jumped up on the table still screaming. So funny. The mouse was harmless and looked so pathetic and frightened. It was definitely hurting and in a panic. I think it finally died and I ended up taking the trap outside, opening the trap and releasing him in the front yard.

One evening I had been visiting my folks on the other side of town. When I walked in my front door and flicked on the light switch, I saw two mice scamper from under the cabinet in the kitchen, one ran under the refrigerator, the other one scrambled around the corner from the bathroom to the refrigerator. I just stood there with my mouth open, pivoted, turned out the light, locked and closed the door, got in my car and went over to my folks place for the night. I was outnumbered!

The next day my brother, Jay, came over to nail some of the holes shut with soup can lids. When he opened the bread drawer, a mouse came running around the rim and went under the cabinet, scaring the b'ejeebers out of him. He reared back on his hind end and let out some expletive. He got a taste of my situation first hand!

I didn't have too much trouble with them after that.

Finally, I took a job up north and the landlord didn't allow animals, so I had to find a home for Rochester. One of the older ladies who fed him hamburger and turkey had recently lost her cat and she willingly took Rochester into her home. I hated to leave him but I had to move on.

Now when I think of Rochester, he brings a smile to my face. He helped me with my mouse problem, sort of. Although he didn't kill any, just the fact that he was there kept them at bay. I felt better about the situation, anyway. I also learned that every seven years field mice propagate like crazy. I just happen to be one lucky (?) recipient of several that season.

Cats, etc.

Just the Cat Facts, Ma'am!
Trivia Tidbits

Did you know?

- Cats have 230 bones in their bodies compared to 206 in a human.

- Cats purr at the frequency of 25 vibrations per second.

- Unlike other vocalizations, purring can occur when inhaling, exhaling and vocalizing. The purr's low vibrations repair bones, relieve pain and promote wound healing.

- Cats can purr as many as 10,950 hours during their lifetime.

- Cats have been known to live as long as 38 years. (Generally 15-20)

- Isaac Newton invented the door flap (access for animals to the outside).

- Sebastian at 3 years old is 28 in human years and Sidney at 2 years old is 24 years old.

- Most cats have no eyelashes. (mine, do)

- Cats eyes are either slanted, almond or round.

- While our average body temperature is 98.6, a cat's is 102.

- A cat's heart beats twice as fast as a human's—155 times a minute.

- A group of kittens is known as a kindle — a group of adult cats are called a clowder.

- A cat can jump between 5 and 7 times as high as he is tall.

- Cats have 8-12 long whiskers on each side of their upper lip. They only lose a few at a time and they have whiskers behind their front legs. Those help the cat land safely and feel for prey.

- Speaking of whiskers, the cats are more than twice as thick as ordinary hairs and their roots are three times deeper.

- Whiskers above the eyes trigger blinking to protect a cat's eyes.

- Kittens in the womb acquire whiskers before body hair.

- Small, rigid projections on the tongue greatly increase its upper surface area so that it can hold more saliva to aid grooming and temperature control

- The rich nerve endings of whiskers register very small changes in air pressure, enabling cats to move adeptly in the dark.

- Cats will sleep between 12-14 hours a day.

- There are 90.5 million cats in North America compared to 74 million dogs.

- Indoor domestic cats live longer than outdoor cats. Outdoor cats may make 5 years.

- Less than 5% of lost cats return home.

- Cats were a sacred animal in ancient Egypt and their history dates back to as early at 8000 years.

- Every year nearly 4 million cats are eaten in Asia.

- Cats are some of the smartest animals and can interpret a human's mood and feelings.

- Cat urine glows in the dark if a black light is shined on it.

- A cat's field of vision is 220 degrees while a humans is 180 degrees.

- Cats have between 20/100 and 20/200 vision at close range.

- A cats vision is sharpest at 2 to 3 feet.

- Cats see black, white, various shades of gray, blue, green and yellow, but not red.

- Cats detect stationary objects poorly, but can observe the slightest movement.

- With cats that have a layer of extra cells to absorb light, cats can see with about 1/6 of the light it takes a human to see.

- A cat's sense of smell is 14 times stronger than ours. It's olfactory membrane is about14 square centimeters compared to 4 square centimeters for humans.

- Cats have about 70 million sent-sensing cells. Humans operate with between 2 million and 20 million.

- Cats have 30 vertebrae while we have 32.

- Cats make about 100 different sounds while dogs make only 10.

- Approximately 1/3 of cat owners think their pets are able to read their minds.

- The little fluffs of hairs in a cat's ear that help keep out dirt and direct sounds into the ear and insulate the ears are called "ear furnishings."

- Cats can give birth to between 1 and 9 kittens. The largest known litter was nineteen; fifteen survived.

- In just seven years, a single pair of cats and their offspring could produce a staggering total of 420,000 kittens.

- A cat called Dusty has the known record for the most kittens. 420 in her lifetime.

- A female cat is called a queen or a molly.

- Cats can detect earthquake tremors 10 to 15 minutes before humans can. They are extremely sensitive to vibrations. Cats hear sounds, especially the can opener or refrigerator opening, four or five times farther away than humans.

- When running at full speed, cats are airborne for most of the extended stride, without any paw touching the ground.

- Pads on the forepaws cushion movement, and the single large pad is the prime shock absorber and anti-skid device.

- Skin on the pads, 70 times thicker than elsewhere on the body, provides further protection.

- Because cats feel safer when everything smells like them, they deposit scent-filled saliva on themselves and on you. I might add here, doorways, or most anything at their level. Cats lap liquids four or five times before swallowing.

- A cat's tongue curls downward when he drinks, throwing liquids into his mouth, not up, which would toss liquids into his face.

- Except for crunching dry food (and your plants), cats do little chewing.

- Cats have 473 taste buds and a less refined sense of taste than humans, who have 9,000 taste buds.

- Cats come in two basic colors, black and red, from which all other colors derive. White is not a color; it hides true color. Many white kittens have a spot of color on their heads that indicates their true color.

- Tabby describes a coat pattern, not a color or breed.

- Tabbies have stripes on their necks, legs and tail and usually have spots on their tummies.

- Tabbies have alternate bands of light and dark color on each hair.

- Tabbies have an "M" on their foreheads; which some people believe stands for mischievous, Mary or Mohammed.

- Cats are digitigrades, meaning they walk on their toes. This lengthens their limbs and reduces contact with the ground, necessities for explosive sprinters.

- Shoulder blades on the sides of the body and a tiny collarbone permit movement in almost every direction and through tight spaces.

- 45% of cats suffer from painful arthritis.

- Only cats, giraffes and camels step with both left legs, then both right legs when they walk or run.

- Claws are actually protractable, not retractable as often described, meaning they are normally hidden until the cat extends them. Claws retract automatically to keep them sharp and allow silent stalking. Front claws are typically sharper than hind claws. Ouch.

- The domestic cat is the only cat species that can hold its tail vertically while walking.

- The tail aids balance and helps maintain orientation during full-speed sharp turns. The tail contains 10 % of a cat's bones.

Sources:

Cat Blessings, a Collection of Poems, Quotes and Myths, by Bob Lovka

The Cat Behavior Answer Book by Arden Moore

Cat Fancy Magazine, May 2010 issue.

Sebastian: "Did you know we're going to be famous some day?"
Sidney: "You don't say... Really?"

Cat Bathing

Tongue in cheek - or- At your own risk

Some people say cats never have to be bathed. They say cats lick themselves clean. They say cats have a special enzyme of some sort in their saliva that works like new, improved Wisk, dislodging the dirt where it hides and whisking it away. I've spent most of my life believing this folklore. Like most blind believers, I've been able to discount all the facts to the contrary, the kitty odors that lurk in the corners of the garage, and dirt smudges that cling to the throw rug by the fireplace. The time comes, however, when a man must face reality; when he must look squarely in the face of massive public sentiment to the contrary and announce: "This cat smells like a port-a-potty on a hot day in Juarez." When that day arrives at your house, as it has in mine, I have some advice you might consider as you place your feline friend under your arm and head for the bathtub.

Know that although the cat has the advantage of quickness and lack of concern for human life, you have the advantage of strength. Capitalize on that advantage by selecting the battlefield. Don't try to bathe him in an open area where he can force you to chase him. Pick a very small bathroom. If the bathroom is more than four feet square, I recommend that you get in the tub with the cat and close the sliding glass doors as if you were about to take a shower. (A simple shower

As printed in the *Orange Peel Gazette–Kane County Edition*

curtain will not do. A berserk cat can shred a three-ply rubber shower curtain quicker than a politician can shift positions.)

Know that a cat has claws and will not hesitate to remove all the skin from your body. Your advantage here is that you are smart and know how to dress to protect yourself. I recommend canvas overalls tucked into high-top construction boots, a pair of steel-mesh gloves, an army helmet, a hockey face mask, and a long-sleeved flak jacket.

Prepare everything in advance. There is no time to go out for a towel when you have a cat digging a hole in your flak jacket. Draw the water. Make sure the bottle of kitty shampoo is inside the glass enclosure. Make sure the towel can be reached, even if you are lying on your back in the water.

Use the element of surprise. Pick up your cat nonchalantly, as if to simply carry him to his supper dish. They have little or no interest in fashion as a rule. (If he does notice your garb, calmly explain that you are taking part in a product testing experiment for J.C. Penney.)

Once you are inside the bathroom, speed is essential to survival. In a single liquid motion, shut the bathroom door, step into the tub enclosure, slide the glass door shut, dip the cat in the water, and squirt him with shampoo. You have begun one of the wildest 45 seconds of your life.

Cats have no handles. Add the fact that he now has soapy fur, and the problem is radically compounded. Do not expect to hold on to him for more than two or three seconds at a time. When you have him, however, you must remember to give him another squirt of shampoo and rub like crazy. He'll then spring free and fall back into the water, thereby rinsing himself off. (The national record for cats is three lathering's, so don't expect too much.)

Next, the cat must be dried. Novice cat bathers always assume this part will be the most difficult, for humans generally are worn out at this point, and the cat is just getting really determined. In fact, the drying is simple compared to what you have just been through. That's because by now the cat is semi-permanently affixed to your right leg. You simply pop the drain plug with your foot, reach for the towel, and wait. (Occasionally, however, the cat will end up clinging to the top of your army helmet. If this happens, the best thing you can do is to shake him loose and to encourage him toward your leg.) After all the water is drained from the tub, it is a simple matter to just reach down and dry the cat.

In a few days, the cat will relax enough to be removed from your leg. He will usually have nothing to say for about three weeks, and will spend a lot of time sitting with his back to you. He might even become psychoceramic and develop the fixed stare of a plaster figurine. You will be tempted to assume he is angry. This isn't usually the case. As a rule, he is simply plotting ways to get through your defenses and injure you for life the next time you decide to give him a bath.

But at least now he smells a lot better.

Cat Sayings
What they mean...and other sayings

"It's raining cats and dogs"
> An expression used to indicate that it's pouring hard and heavy

"Curiosity killed the cat"
> A phrase used as a cautionary expression. To mind your own business.

"Let the cat out of the bag"
> To spill the beans-so to speak.

"Sick as a cat"
> Cats are known for hiding any sign of illness, so when they appear to be sick it usually means that their ailment might be quite advanced. The phrase suggests that a person is very sick.

"To fight like cats and dogs"
> This phrase means the legendary animosity between cats and dogs. No holds barred kind of battle.

"To be like a cat on a hot tin roof"
> To be excited and nervous.

"To grin like a Cheshire cat"
> To display a very big mischievous smile. The exact origins of this saying is not exactly known, but it has been widely associated with the adventures of Alice in Wonderland, by Lewis Carroll, and the equally famous Cheshire cat.

"Like herding cats"
> An almost impossible task.

"Dogs have owners, cats have staff"
> Pretty much self-explanatory.

Cat sayings can contain so much wisdom--Cats, many great thinkers have said, make fantastic philosophers. Just watch a cat and you are sure to see the world in a brand new way.

"A cat is a cat...and that is that!"

"A house is not a home until it has a cat..."

"A cat has nine lives."
> The short version; Cats are more tenacious of life than other animals. The long version; There were nine Gods collectively known as the Ennead or the nine. The priesthood of On worshipped Atum Ra, a sun god and took the form of a cat embodying nine lives in one creator.

"Cat got your tongue?"

"Dogs remember faces; cat's places."

"Fat cat"
> refers to a rich and influential person

"He (or she) is a cool cat"

"He looks like a cat who swallowed the canary."

"There is more than one way to skin a cat."

"It would make a cat laugh."
> An Irish saying when something is funny.

"If stretching were wealth, the cat would be rich"
> African saying

"In the dark, all cats are gray."

"Look what the cat dragged in."

"Nervous as a cat in a room full of rocking chairs."

"Not a cat in hell's chance."

"The cat wonders at it's own tail."
> Spanish saying

"The dog for the man, the cat for the woman."

"When you want to play, cats want to be left alone."

"Who would believe such pleasure from a wee ball o' fur?"
> Irish saying

Cat Quotes

"If God created man in his own image, you've got to wonder, in whose image did he create the nobler cat?"

Unknown

"Essentially, you do not so much teach your cat as you bribe him."

Lynn Holly

"There are few things in life more heart warming than to be welcomed by a cat."

Tay Hohoff

"It is remarkable, in cats, that the outer life they reveal to their masters is one of perpetual boredom."

Robley Wilson, Jr.

"Way down deep we are all motivated by the same urges, cats have the courage to live by them."

Jim Davis

"Two cats can live as cheaply as one, and their owner has twice as much fun."

Lloyd Alexander

"There is no cat "language." Painful as it is for us to admit, they don't need one."

Barbara Holland

"Time spent with cats is never wasted."

May Sarton

"The furry little buggers (cats) are just deep, deep wells
you throw your emotions into."

Bruce Schimmel

"Cats can work out mathematically the exact place to sit that will
cause most inconvenience."

Pam Brown

"Cats have an infallible understanding of total concentration—
and get between you and it."

Arthur Bridges

"A kitten is so flexible that she is almost double the hind parts are
equivalent to another kitten with which the forepart plays. She does
not discover that her tail belongs to her until you tread on it."

Henry David Thoreau

"…You are my cat and I am your human. "

Hilaire Belloc

"Dogs eat. Cats dine"

Ann Taylor

"Every life should have nine cats."

Anonymous

"If cats could talk, they wouldn't."

Nan Porter

"If the pull of the outside world is strong, there is also a pull towards
the human. The cat may disappear on its own errands, but sooner or
later, it returns once again for a little while, to greet us with it's own
type of love. Independent as they are, cats find more than pleasure in
our company."

Lloyd Alexander

"Cats were put into the world to disprove the dogma that all things
were created to serve man."

Paul Gray

"To err is human, to purr is feline."

Robert Byrne

"The smallest feline is a masterpiece."

Leonardo Da Vinci

"Our perfect companions never have fewer than four feet."

Colette

"The ideal calm exists in a sitting cat."

Jules Reynard

Cat Proverbs

"You will always be lucky if you know how to make
friends with strange cats."

Colonial Proverb

"In a cat's eye, all things belong to cats."

English Proverb

"Beware of people who dislike cats."

Irish Proverb

"After dark all cats are leopards."

Native American Proverb

Happy owner, happy cat. Indifferent owner, reclusive cat.

Chinese Proverb

A cat has nine lives. For three he plays, for three he strays,
and for the rest three he stays.

English Proverb

"Happy is the home with at least one cat."

Italian Proverb

"Books and cats and fair-haired little girls make the best furnishings
for a room."

French Proverb

"The cat who frightens the mice away is as good as the cat who eats
them."

German Proverb

Sebastian and Me

"A cat bitten once by a snake dreads even rope."

Arab Proverb

"The cat is nature's Beauty."

French Proverb

"When rats infest the Palace a lame cat is better than the swiftest horse."

Chinese Proverb

"A cornered cat becomes as fierce as a lion."

"If you don't feed the cats you must feed the rats."

Cat Superstitions

To reverse the bad luck curse of a black cat crossing your path, first walk in a circle, then go backward across the spot where it happened and count to 13.

Dreaming of a white cat means good luck.

American superstition

It is bad luck to see a white cat at night.

American superstition

A strange black cat on your porch brings prosperity.

Scottish superstition

If a cat washes behinds its ears, it will rain.

English superstition

A cat sneezing is a good omen for everyone who hears it.

Italian superstition

When moving to a new home, always put the cat through the window instead of the door, so that it will not leave.

American superstition

In the Netherlands, cats were not allowed in rooms where private family discussions were going on. The Dutch believed that cats would definitely spread gossip around the town.

Netherlands superstition.

When you see a one-eyed cat, spit on your thumb, stamp it in the palm of your hand, and make a wish. The wish will come true.

American superstition

Cats are Bringers of Good Luck:

In Scotland, some believed that a black kitten on the porch meant future happiness and Riches.

Other indicators of good luck have included:

A cat at a wedding

A sneezing cat

Dreaming of a white cat

A black cat crossing one's path (UK, Japan)

A black cat walking toward a person

Japan's Maneko Neko, or "good luck cat" is a beckoning feline with one paw raised that is said to bring good fortune. As it is believed to invite wealth, piggy banks are often created in the shape of the Maneko Neko.

Cats as Harbingers of Bad Luck:

At various times and in various places, the following have been considered bad luck:
Seeing a white cat at night

A black cat walking toward a person but then stopping and turning away.

Chasing a black cat out of one's home

Although having a black cat cross one's path is considered bad luck in America and various European countries outside the UK, in Germany, if the black cat crosses from left to right, it portends good luck (crossing in the other direction indicates bad luck).

Superstitions Regarding Health and Safety:

Throughout the ages, there have been various superstitions regarding cats and health, including:

One who kicks a cat will develop rheumatism in that leg.

A black cat lying on a sick person's bed will bring death.

Stroking a black cat will ensure health and wealth.

Cats will suck the breath from babies.

Myths involving cats and the safety of boats at sea are also quite common.

In certain fishing communities, the wives of fisherman will keep cats indoors, as this is believed to protect their men from peril at sea.

Sailors once thought that throwing a cat overboard would cause their ship to sink in a storm.

Beliefs Regarding the Ability of Cats to Predict the Weather:

In the past, many believed that cat behaviors could predict weather. For example:

A cat licking its tail or washing behind its ears meant that rain was on its way.

A restless cat indicated that a storm was brewing.

When a cat pointed its tail toward the fireplace, bad weather would follow shortly thereafter.

Pouring or sprinkling water on a cat would make it rain.

Myths Regarding Cats and Evil Spirits:

People of various cultures at various times throughout history have believed that cats are goblins, vampires, fairies, or sorcerers in disguise. Some additional examples of Superstitions linking cats to evil entities include:

Drown a cat and the Devil will get you.

If a cat leaps over a corpse, the dead body will reanimate as a vampire.

Mummifying a cat and placing it inside a wall will ward off evil spirits.

Positive Feline Spiritual Associations:
Cats have also been linked with positive spiritual beliefs, the best known of which is the Egyptian reverence for felines. Other examples include:

Latvia, where a black cat in a grain silo is a good thing because these cats are the manifestation of the harvest god Rungis.

Japan, where a cat with a black spot on its fur embodies the soul of a dead ancestor.

Deities that could assume the form of a cat have included:
the goddess Diana in Rome

the god Ai Apaec in Peru

the deity Li Shou in china, which had the power to ward off evil spirits

In Burma and Siam, when a holy man died, it was believed that his spirit would enter a cat. Then, when the cat died, his spirit was transported to paradise.

In Scandinavia, the goddess Freyja rode a cat-drawn chariot, and farmers would leave offerings for Freyja's cats so that their harvests would be bountiful.

Similar ideas regarding cats and fertility led some Europeans to decorate cats with ribbons and send them into fields after the harvest to appease the gods.

Other Cat-Related Superstitions:

A few other amusing beliefs regarding cats have included the following:

If a cat washes itself, company is coming.

Upon seeing a one-eyed cat, a person should make a wish, then spit on his thumb and stamp it into the palm of his hand so that the wish will come true.

Pregnant women should not allow cats to sleep on their laps, or their babies may be born with cat faces.

Cats are Neither Lucky nor Unlucky

The reality is that cats have no effect on luck or weather, though they actually do bring certain health benefits to their owners. However, superstitions about cats persist, many of them stemming from the time of the witch hunts.

Lighten Up
Cat jokes

Did you hear about the cat who drank five bowls of water?
> He set a new lap record.

Did you hear about the cat who swallowed a ball of wool?
> She had mittens.

What is the difference between a cat and a comma?
> One has the paws before the claws and the other has the
> clause before the pause.

What do you get when you cross a chick with an alley cat?
> A peeping tom.

Why don't cats play poker in the jungle?
> Too many cheetahs.

What is a cat's favorite song?
> Three Blind Mice.

What is a cat's way of keeping law & order?
> Claw Enforcement.

How did a cat take first prize at the bird show?
> He jumped up to the cage, reached in and took it.

Why did a person with an unsprayed female cat have to go to court?
> For kitty littering.

Why did the litter of communist kittens become capitalists?
> Because they finally opened their eyes.

Sebastian and Me

Why are cats better than babies?

     Because you only have to change a litter box once a day.

What is the name of the unauthorized autobiography of the cat?

     Hiss and tell.

Top 5 Funny Cat Jokes

Funny Cat Joke #1:

A man absolutely hated his wife's cat and decided to get rid of him one day by driving him 20 blocks from his home and leaving him at the park. As he arrived home, the cat was walking up the driveway.

The next day he decided to drive the cat 40 blocks away. He put the beast out and headed home. Driving back up his driveway, there was the cat!

He kept taking the cat further and further, and the cat would always beat him home. At last he decided to drive a few miles away, turn right, then left, past the bridge, then right again and another right until he reached what he thought was a safe distance from his home and left the cat there.

Hours later the man calls home to his wife.. "Jen, is the cat there?"

"Yes." the wife answers. "why do you ask?"

Frustrated, the man answered, "Put the little bastard on the phone. I'm lost and need directions."

Funny Cat Joke #2:

One day a cat dies of natural causes and goes to Heaven. There he meets the Lord himself.

The Lord says to the cat, "You lived a good life and if there is any way I can make your stay in Heaven more comfortable, please let me know."

The cat thinks for a moment and says, "Lord, all my life I have lived with a poor family and had to sleep on a hard wooden floor."

The Lord stops the cat and says, "Say no more," and a wonderful fluffy pillow appears.

A few days later six mice are killed in a tragic farming accident and go to Heaven. Again the Lord is there to greet them with the same offer.

The mice answer, "All of our lives we have been chased. We have had to run from cats, dogs, and even women with brooms. Running, running, running; we're tired of running. Do you think we could have roller skates so we don't have to run anymore?"

The Lord says, "Say no more," and fits each mouse with beautiful new roller skates.

About a week later the Lord stops by to see the cat and finds him in a deep sleep on the pillow.

The Lord gently wakes the cat and asks him, "How are things since you arrived?"

The cat stretches and yawns and replies, "It is wonderful here. Better than I could have ever expected. And those Meals on Wheels you've been sending by are theeeeeee best!!!"

Funny Cat Joke #3:

A mother cat was teaching her kitten cat lore. She explained that this was the duty of all mother cats since before recorded history and it was important that her kitten would not do anything to embarrass her when she allowed her master to play with her.

At the end of the lesson, after she had gone over all the cat rules such as ignoring anything the human might say, she asked her kitten if there was a question she might want to ask.

The kitten said, "Momma, you have told me all the situations a cat might get into and the proper cat-responses but, what should I do if a new situation comes up that you haven't covered"?

Momma cat responded, "Oh my gosh! I'm SO glad you asked that. I've gotten into so many rules that I forgot the most important first rule!"

Kitten asked: "What is that, Momma?"

Momma drew up and looked kitten right in the eye and said: "When in doubt ---wash!"

Funny Cat Joke #4:

A man runs into the vet's office carrying his dog, screaming for help. The vet rushes him back to an examination room and has him put his dog down on the examination table. The vet examines the still, limp body and after a few moments, tells the man that his dog, regrettably, is dead. The man, clearly agitated and not willing to accept this, demands a second opinion. The vet goes into the back room and comes out with a cat and puts the cat down next to the dog's body. The cat sniffs the body, walks from head to tail, poking and sniffing the dog's body and finally looks at the vet and meows.

The vet looks at the man and says, "I'm sorry, but the cat thinks that your dog is dead, too."

The man, finally resigned to the diagnosis, thanks the vet and asks how much he owes. The vet answers, "$350."

"$350 to tell me my dog is dead?!" exclaims the man.

"Well," the vet replies, "I would only have charged you $50 for my initial diagnosis. The additional $300 was for the cat scan."

Funny Cat Joke #5:

A couple were out for the evening. They'd gotten ready, all dolled up, cat put out, etc...

The taxi arrives and as the couple go out, the cat shoots back in. They don't want the cat shut in the house, so the wife goes out to the taxi while the husband goes upstairs to chase the cat out.

The wife, not wanting it known that the house will be empty, explains to the taxi driver, ... "He's just going upstairs to say goodbye to my mother."

A few minutes later, the husband gets into the cab: "sorry I took so long," he says, "stupid old thing was hiding under the bed and I had to poke her with a coat hanger to get her to come out!"

The taxi driver.....????!!!!@#!@!-#$#$%@

The Interview
Why write a book?

"Why not?"
Kay Clark

It was a brisk December day. Familiar songs of the holiday season softly filled the room and my small apartment from the stereo. Sebastian and Sidney were comfortably curled up on the loveseat snoozing away. And I was nervously seated on my red sofa waiting for the interviewer to arrive and discuss my first published book, *Sebastian and Me; A Rite of Passage and Spiritual Journey.* In front of me was a tray with a pot of hot tea, two cups, cloth napkins, and on a small dish, warm, freshly baked, sliced banana bread. A small tub of margarine, honey and some sugars nearby. I glanced at my watch.

There was the buzzer to the door. It was the interviewer. Right on time.

"Come on up," I invited after I pushed the button on the intercom.

She made her way up the stairs and saw me peering out of the door to my apartment.

"Hi, how are you?" I asked in a friendly tone.

"I'm-just-fine." She responded almost breathless.

"I think they added a few more steps than normal." I offered to help her feel at ease.

"May I take your coat?" Sidney, on alert now, jumped down off the loveseat and scampered into the bedroom and under my bed while Sebastian stretched and checked out our visitor.

"Oh yes, thank you." And I helped her out of her coat hanging it up in the closet.

"Go on in and make yourself comfortable. Have a seat there on the sofa. Would you like a cup of tea? Help yourself to the goodies. I hope you're not allergic to cats." I said closing the coat closet door.

"Oh no. A hot cup of tea sounds wonderful. Thank you." She was grateful for the offer. "What a beautiful cat. Is this Sebastian?"

She set her purse down, and placed her note-book in her lap making herself comfortable while I poured a cup of tea.

"Yes, that's him. My little sweetheart. Honey or sugar?" I added. "Sidney is out of sight. She's rather skittish around people. She's probably under my bed."

"Honey." She rubbed her hands together briskly as I poured some honey into the steaming cup.

"Thank you. It's chilly out there today. Have you been out?" she asked and stirred her tea.

"Yes, that wind doesn't help." I responded. It was a wintry day and it was December.

"Ok, let's get started." The interviewer was eager to make the most of our time together. I appreciated that.

INTERVIEWER: "So tell me, Kay, how did you come about becoming a writer?"

K: "I believe it was in Junior High English class. We were asked to write a story and when I got the paper back the teacher made some very positive comments and gave me an "A." "A's" in her class were hard to come by so I was quite pleased. That planted a seed in me. Later on in high school, I would write romantic scenarios involving my classmates. Something like soap operas. I just knew I wanted to write a book someday. About what, I wasn't sure."

INTERVIEWER: "And what made you want to write about your cats?"

K: "Sebastian came into my life when I needed a companion. Sometimes animals, and especially cats, are more readily available than a good man. (chuckle.) I had been living alone after having left my marriage and when I moved away a lot of things changed. Now it was just him and I. We had already formed a bond and sort of depended on one another for emotional support and when he took off, I'd lost my Heaven-sent Band-Aid."

INTERVIEWER: "Some people would wonder why you were so tied to Sebastian."

K: "Yes, I can understand that, too. Being single and alone, losing my job, then bonding with him with all of that spare time, then with the loss of my father, and then the car accident, …when he left I was feeling rather lost myself."

INTERVIEWER: "Why did you write the part about him being 'Gone' as in a journal or diary form?"

K: "I look upon it as a cathartic adventure. I needed to work through my anxiety by recording my thoughts of loss and then by physically going out and searching for him. I mean, I was out of work and needed the exercise anyway and it seemed no one was hiring so what better way to work through some of those issues?"

INTERVIEWER: "Ah…makes sense now. I see you took particular pleasure in describing their antics. You really love these two, don't you?"

K: "Well, yes, they are so cute and cuddly. Besides being entertaining. Sebastian in particular is the more affectionate one. Do you have pets?"

INTERVIEWER: "No. My apartment doesn't allow pets. I see you also included several photos of your cats. Do you have an interest in photography as well?"

K: "Yes, I do. In fact, I've had several of my photos on display in a few places in Elgin and in Platteville, Wisconsin, my home town. It's another hobby of mine. A few have even sold, but then I'm just getting them out there."

INTERVIEWER: "Very nice. From your Junior High school days until now, there have been several years in between. What made you finally decide to jump back into writing?"

K: "Oh! Well, for several years I was sending out Christmas letters. I know some people groan when they open those at Christmas, but one lady friend took the time to call and praise me for how well it was written. Several others have commented on my skill also, and that has given me the impetus to really do something about it. And then a couple of years ago, I learned of the Algonquin Area Writer's Group. It has helped me immeasurably in honing my skill and I try never to miss a meeting. Through the members' positive critiques of my work, it's given me the confidence to take that next step. That, and the influence of Carolyn Batzlaff, a lady friend I met through the group. She had convinced me to accept this writing challenge. She's on her third book. I'm so proud of her. She's my role model and mentor. We continue our meeting afterward and encourage and inspire one another. She's really a great friend and I'm pleased to have met her through the group.

INTERVIEWER: "Had you expected your book to be the success that it has been?"

K: "No! But I'm certainly pleased that it has done so well so far! There are more cat owners than dog owners. And of course, I have dreams of it being on the Best Seller List. (She chuckles with anticipation.)

INTERVIEWER: "What are your plans for the future?"

K: "I'd like to write another one. I'm thinking of writing about wedding proposals. I've always wondered how people have met and then to learn of their courtships and romantic proposals. I think we all need more romance in our lives. Don't you agree?"

INTERVIEWER: "Oh yes!" She agreed and grinned widely. After a short pause she continued the interview by asking, "And whom do you aspire to?"

K: "To be another J. K. Rowling or Stephen King." Kay breaks out in laughter. "Why not shoot for the moon? At least you'll land among the stars. That's what they say, anyway, right?" She breaks out in laughter again with a twinkle in her eye.

INTERVIEWER: "Any parting thoughts or advice for those thinking of trying their hand at writing and publishing a book?"

K: "First off, I'm self-published, so I'm not going through an agent or big publishing house. Just as a good photographer keeps her camera close by, I'd keep a notebook and pen handy, too. Jot down little snippets of thoughts or phrases. Sometimes your best ideas come to you just before you drop off to sleep or even in your dreams. A notebook next to your bed is a good idea.

I would advise not letting go of your dreams. Some people advise you try to write a little every day. Join a writing group. And also, call on your Writing Angel to help you if you get in a bind. Be positive. In fact, I've already been practicing on how I would sign the front page at the book signings, "Believe in the Power of your Dreams. - Kay Clark'

INTERVIEWER: "Well, that's positive thinking! I wish you all the best of luck on your first book, Kay."

K: "Thank you. And thank you for your time."

Made in the USA
Charleston, SC
24 October 2012